LIVED TO TELL
THRIVING AFTER SUICIDE ATTEMPT

Thank you for picking up my book. Please enjoy.

Kay Whiting Harrison
with Wendy O'Leary

Kay W. Harrison

NLKC
Publishing

ISBN 979-888722937-9

Published by NLKC Publishing
thrivingaftersuicideattempt@gmail.com
www.thrivingaftersuicideattempt.com

Cover Design: Anne Whiting Richardson
Co-Writer: Wendy O'Leary
Copyeditor: Tish Dahmen

NOTE: The contents of this book are based upon the author's personal experiences with mental illness and suicidal thoughts. The insights, advice and resources provided herein are not intended to be a substitute for professional treatment. If you are experiencing suicidal thoughts, please reach out and talk to someone immediately or call the national suicide hotline # 988 (if not available in your area, please call 800.273.8255).

In Praise of

Lived to Tell: Thriving After Suicide Attempt

"I believe that most people will relate to Kay's story as it is not only about overcoming stigma and hopelessness relating to mental illness, but how we cope when life doesn't give us what we expected. Through Kay's story we see the value in sharing our own stories. As we are honest with others about our feelings and our mental health, we are able to rally a support network that can professionally and emotionally support us through the overwhelming challenges that we will all encounter in our lives. Thank you, Kay, for your immense courage in sharing your story. Brave and relatable, vulnerable and strong." ~ **Karen Marriott, Community Advocate, Park City, Utah.**

"WOW!!! I read the book cover to cover. I couldn't put it down! It's a great story and reinforces the truism that we need to stop hiding mental illness, share our struggles, talk about it, and get rid of the stigma surrounding it, or nothing will change and countless lives will be lost and families devastated. This book is well-written and flows very smoothly. As I said, I couldn't put it down. I truly believe this book will help many, many people. People who are overwhelmed, afraid, feeling shame, who don't know where to turn. I'm glad she survived and is here to help others!" ~ **Kathy Grieve, former NAMI Utah Affiliate Leader and NAMI Basics Teacher**

"Thank you for letting me read this manuscript. It is beautiful to see the recovery process in someone's life. As a seasoned psychiatric nurse, it gave me a new awareness of how the stigma of mental illness can hinder people from seeking treatment and how this can be potentially deadly. This is a touching story of Kay's struggles, detailed enough that you really get a sense of who she is, a professional woman, a loving mother and a wife who has weathered many storms. Yet through it all she did not disclose how much she was suffering and the depths of her depression. Kay's story contradicts the stigma that people with mental illness aren't strong. In the end she achieved one the highest levels of recovery, being an advocate for others with mental illness. It is written well and at times I was convicted by some of my own stigma, as I don't know if I could have gone through all she went through, and then turn around and become a champion advocate for others." ~ **Lee Ann Brunson, Psychiatric Nurse at Veterans Administration SLC, Utah**

"This is a poignant tale of darkness that didn't lead to defeat. Everyone should spend a minute with Kay and the pages of her story because either they know someone - or they are someone - who is suffering. Most of us don't know how to step off of the gerbil wheel of stress, anxiety, depression, grief and shame and into the world we all deserve. A world of peace and happiness. Kay shows us how we can do this." ~ **Lisa Cook, Author of 'Grit, Grace and Gratitude' and soon to be released, "Unfolding: A Beginner's Guide to Caring for the Soul." Lisa has personally experienced the devastating loss of her husband to serious mental illness and suicide.**

"Kay Harrison's book is a powerful and wonderfully sensitive account of what it's like to suffer from depression and a very serious attempt at suicide. It will benefit many people in this country who suffer from depression as well as their loved ones and friends who want to help. Its compassion, along with her account of practical problem-solving solutions is humble yet immensely helpful. Although it is not a "how to" book, it provides insight into the mind and heart of sufferers of this often-deadly disorder and strategies to recover and thrive." ~ **Dr. Xavier Amador, Ph.D. An internationally sought-after speaker and trainer, clinical psychologist, professor, author, and founder of the LEAP Institute.**

"Having read this book several times now, I can honestly say it is an incredible story. Each time I read it I find something new jumps out at me. It is an honest raw depiction of Kay and the things she has dealt with her entire life. As I read I find myself in her shoes going through all the emotions. You cannot put it down. I love hearing from Lex and getting his point of view. So much of this book spoke to me as I'm sure it will to many others who deal with depression, anxiety and other mental illnesses. It is the right time and season for this book. I commend Kay for sharing her story with the world. If it helps just one person it will be worth it but I am sure it will help many!" ~ **Marie Crook Watkins, Book Lover, Avid Reader and Librarian 10+ Years**

"I broke down and cried as I read the part leading up to and culminating in her suicide attempt and her husband finding her and his reaction. I know how ruminating and spiraling downward feels. For those of us who have suicidal ideation, this lady's story is so relatable. This is a wonderful book that will help people understand. Her story takes on a universal problem. Kay had a tough road and understandably thought she couldn't share her troubled feelings and thoughts. This story can teach us that when we step forward into the light and send that light in a circle around us, then we can begin to heal. That is what happened to Kay as she learned not to hide alone in the dark anymore. It's so important to have validating people who listen and can be empathetic. Each person's journey is private and Kay could have kept her story private, too. I am thankful she chose to write her story because I think it will help a lot of people - I'm guessing it already has. Everyone who has these experiences either become their own heroes or they fall prey to more trauma. This is a touching story and I couldn't put it down." ~ **Gayle Hollingsworth, State of Utah Certified Peer Support Specialist, NAMI Utah Teacher and Support Group Facilitator, long time NAMI Utah Board Member**

Dedicated to
my incredible family

My husband, Lex
and
my children,
Naquel
Lacy / Matt
Kallie
Chase / Brittney

Thank you for your unconditional love.

This is not easy,
This recovery of yours.
But you are here
And still working,
Still growing.

You have triumphed
Over dark.
You are strong.
Be proud.
You are here.

~ Kay Whiting Harrison ~

TABLE OF CONTENTS

PART TWO. Advice and Resources

FORWARD

Kay Harrison's book is a powerful and wonderfully sensitive account of what it's like to suffer from depression and a very serious attempt at suicide. It will benefit many people in this country who suffer from depression as well as their loved ones and friends who want to help. Its compassion, along with her account of practical problem-solving solutions is humble yet immensely helpful. Although it is not a "how to" book, it provides insight into the mind and heart of sufferers of this often-deadly disorder and strategies to recover and thrive.

In this book you will read about a childhood that was blessed with many things including loving parents and no signs of the life-threatening hurdles that lay ahead of her. You will learn of her strong and loving relationship with her husband Lex and the ways in which they cared for their severely disabled daughter and how Kay stepped up and cared for their twelve-year-old son who was diagnosed with cancer. Kay was strong, determined and able to handle the devastation of their daughter's severe terminal disability and the terror of a young son with cancer. We learn about the joy she derived from mothering all of her children, and how her surviving children grew into productive and healthy adults. Her life's story offers no clue of what was to come.

What came was Major Depressive Disorder, coupled with thoughts of suicide, followed by a very serious attempt from which she died but was miraculously revived by her husband. The rate of death by suicide in this country, for persons with the disorder Kay ultimately suffered from, hovers around ten percent. The mortality rate by suicide is higher than most forms of cancer. Yet this illness and the death it too frequently results in, is often swept under the rug, ignored and dismissed...until it is too late.

Her husband's story is part of this book. He writes from the heart and reveals the confusion that comes with living with someone who is depressed and stigmatized. He writes eloquently and offers profound insights into what it is like to care for a loved one who is depressed. His best efforts did not relieve her depression because, like many sufferers, she often tried to hide how she was feeling from him. Though not fully understanding the seriousness of her illness, Lex was instrumental in saving her life after the attempted suicide. The account of Kay's suicide attempt and Lex's resuscitation of his wife, followed by his care of her afterwards is as riveting as it is touching.

Kay writes movingly about what it is like to suffer from long-term depression and the stigma associated with this disease. She writes, "I thought my mood swings were a sign that I had something wrong with me - a character defect or weakness that I couldn't overcome." This book will help all readers to overcome the stigma and seek help. Her account of the suicide attempt and the days leading up to it are profoundly honest and vulnerable. How her husband literally saved her life is miraculous. Kay has turned /tragedy into victory and provides a vision and insight into how the darkest of days, the worst times in life, can yield to a rising sun of hope and a life well lived. The last chapters shine with hope and clarity as we see how Kay and her family are not only surviving her depression and near death by suicide, but also thriving.

I give this book my highest recommendation. It will help persons suffering from this devastating illness, their loved one, their friends and the general public. It is a must read for those with depression and those that want to help.

Xavier Amador, Ph.D.

Professor of Psychiatry and Psychology, University of Utah, and President of The LEAP Institute. Past Board member of the National Alliance on Mental Illness, Professor and Director of Psychology at Columbia University College of Physicians and Surgeons, Director of Psychology at the New York State Psychiatric Institute and author of the following books: *When Someone You Love is Depressed, How to Help Without Losing Yourself*, *Break the Bipolar Cycle*, *I Am Not Sick, I Don't Need Help! How to Help Someone with Mental Illness Accept Treatment*, *Insight and Psychosis; Awareness of Illness in Schizophrenia and Related Disorders*, *I'm Right, You're Wrong. Now What? Break the Impasse and Get What You Need.*

INTRODUCTION

————— ◆ —————

"One day you will tell your story of how you've overcome what you are going through now and it will become part of someone else's survival guide."

~ Brene Brown

In the pages that follow, you will learn about my life's journey and how mental illness weaved its way into and around my thinking and actions. You will get a peek inside the mind and heart of someone who tried very hard to keep it together and how my struggle with mental illness culminated in an attempt to end my own life. You will see the rocky road that led to my recovery and healing journey. I do not profess to have the answers for you or your loved one. Nor do I think everyone's journey will look like mine. It's still not easy to share some of the details of my life knowing that they don't always paint a pretty picture. But if it helps even one person, it will be well worth the discomfort.

Suicide and mental illness are tough topics. They are not easy to talk about especially when they hit close to home – when you are struggling with mental or emotional stress or if you have thoughts about taking your own life. It's frightening when you love someone who is struggling with symptoms of mental illness. It's terrifying when your loved one has contemplated or perhaps attempted suicide. There is a feeling of powerlessness. You can be overwhelmed by the many possible and terrible outcomes associated with mental illness. It's not easy to talk about these things, but it's absolutely essential.

I often talk to individuals and give talks to small and large audiences about my experience. I find that in sharing my story of mental illness, my suicide attempt, and my recovery journey, it has given others permission to finally open up and share their own pain, fear, and struggles - sometimes for the very first time. I talk to people who have kept their struggles with depression and anxiety locked inside of them for years. I talk to family members who are feeling helpless and anxious about someone they love who refuses to get help for their depression or anxiety or other mental health symptoms.

This trajectory of my life makes sense because, as someone recently pointed out, I've gathered people together from all walks of life and socio-economic backgrounds around common goals and/or events – including charitable work, nonprofit causes, business events, chamber of commerce members, or throwing large or small parties. Without being aware, I've become a gatherer. Now, it seems, I am a gatherer of people whose hearts are heavy and minds confused due to their own or a loved one's mental illness.

So, thank you for picking up this book and reading about something that is difficult. I hope that you will find something beneficial here that will help you on your journey. I hope you will take away at least one nugget or one piece of information that makes a difference in your life or in the life of someone you care about.

"You never know how strong you are until being strong is your only choice."

~ Bob Marley

IN THE BEGINNING

————— ◆ —————

"You can't control the cards you're dealt, just how you play the hand."

~ Randy Pausch

I grew up in a small town nestled in the beautiful mountains of Utah. Being surrounded by several major ski resorts and the "Greatest Snow on Earth" I became an avid skier at a young age. I met and married my husband, Lex, while in college. We were racing together on a university ski team. We were both in love with the mountains, the snow, the skiing and each other. I was studying early childhood development and Lex was studying business. He also earned gemological degrees and certifications. He was preparing to take over his family's jewelry business and I was going to raise our future children. We were ready for our happily ever after!

That was the plan. We knew there would be problems and challenges but we didn't anticipate the unimaginable depth of heartbreak and tragedy that would be ours to bear. Nor did we know that the dark clouds of mental illness would hover over us so persistently for so long. I've often said that if someone handed me the script for my life before getting married, I would have handed it back saying, "No thank you. You have the wrong person. I could never bear those trials! You've got to give this to a stronger woman than me!"

Hindsight is 20/20. Looking back, I now realize there were things that happened to me early on as a child that affected my mental health. I was bullied by a kid in my neighborhood. One of the impacts of bullying is decreased self-confidence. This was true for me. I sometimes doubted my own abilities which created a fear of showing up fully in school. Although I was popular enough, active, and had friends, I didn't put myself out there like I wanted to. I held back. As a result, I didn't experience my full potential during junior and senior high school.

Another huge influence on my life was my good childhood friend, Claude Hicken. Although I wouldn't realize or cherish his influence until much later, he became an important person in my life. He was funny and always up to some humorous mischief. I was amused and impressed at how he could talk us out of trouble with the principal after we were caught talking excessively during class. I lost touch with Claude, and many of my classmates, after graduation when we went our separate ways.

Lex and I were young, healthy, full of optimism and faith as we stepped into our lives together as a married couple. We were excited about starting a family.

"Be true to your convictions, and do not settle. You may take some detours and encounter some roadblocks along the way, but never give up on the pursuit of excellence—however you may define that for yourself." ~ Elaine Welteroth

FIRST BORN

————◆————

"I want to tell you that I'll love you forever. Not just yesterday, today, or tomorrow, but every single day for the rest of the eternities."

~ Kay Whiting Harrison

When our first child was born, Naquel, (pronounced Na-kel) I felt complete. I was blessed with everything I had ever wanted – a loving husband, a comfortable home, friends and family who loved us, and now my first child. I knew in my heart I would be a loving and fabulous mother.

The "model-mother" story didn't last long. Within a few short weeks, my precious baby was having seizures. My mothering skills were being challenged daily – and I was coming up short. I didn't know what to do for my baby. I was devastated but also determined to find answers. So began my new role as 'Turbo-Mother' - the mother who exhausted every medical avenue across the western United States and explored every alternative healing modality available to find a cure that would save her child.

Naquel Anne was named after my sister, Anne, whom I adore and cherish. It was during one of Anne's early visits that Naquel first stopped breathing, slumped over lifelessly and started to turn blue. She resumed breathing within a minute but we still rushed her to the hospital where she was thoroughly checked out and sent back home with the assurance that all was well. But it was not. Naquel started having seizures within the week and shortly afterward we took her on a round of doctors and hospitals in search of answers. Her seizures were terrifying. She would stop breathing, go completely limp – lifeless – and then suddenly start breathing again.

During one of our many visits to our pediatrician's office he asked if we would like to speak to the pediatric psychologist. We did. We valued his counsel, specifically one take-away that I appreciate to this day. He said, "Every emotion and feeling you are experiencing right now with your daughter is perfectly normal. You might be angry with each other, with God, with family members or friends. What you need to remember is that these are all natural reactions to your circumstances and it's okay to be upset. What I caution you about is getting stuck in any of these emotional states. If that happens and can't move through it, it is important to seek professional help." What I also remember vividly is him telling us that the average divorce rate for parents of a sick or handicapped child is 75 percent and this was in the late 1970's!

At seven months old, after several types of seizure patterns, seizure medications, family upheavals, emotional breakdowns, more doctors, more hospitals, more tests, and despite the grave prognosis we had been given about her prospects for recovery, I felt optimistic about her progress. I still believed she would recover. I remember being excited when at six months old she was lying on her tummy and pushing her head up. Her seizures had been less frequent and less severe. One day she even rolled from her tummy to her back. I was ecstatic and filled with hope.

Taking Naquel out in public, to church or other places, was emotionally draining. Her seizures were not small or unnoticeable. Her little body would stiffen up and extend into a painfully contorted stretch followed by involuntary spasms. Her entire body would start jerking - abdomen, head, neck, arms and legs. Through each seizure, Naquel whimpered and gasped for air. Each spasm would last for a couple of seconds. Usually, one followed another every five or ten seconds until the cluster of spasms would subside. Each episode would last anywhere from a few minutes to an hour. After a seizure her tiny body would go limp and she would fall asleep exhausted, unless another seizure occurred, which happened too often, and she would begin convulsing again.

When in public, it was too difficult, maybe impossible, to try to explain to observers what was happening. It was easier to escape to the privacy of my car, holding my sweet baby close to my heart, sobbing and wishing I could stop these debilitating seizures. When Naquel was a little over one year old, I counted 100 seizures in one day. Each episode was overwhelmingly painful and heartbreaking for me as a mother. It's something you never "get used to".

Fortunately, Lex and I lived in a wonderful neighborhood and there were some teen girls who became acquainted with Naquel. Remarkably, they wanted to spend time with her, loving her and adoring her, despite her condition. Once they became familiar with the seizures and what to do, they were not afraid to be with her. They wanted instead to hold her and comfort her. These young girls became experts in caring for Naquel. They would watch her, giving me a chance to catch up on housework. Sometimes they and their mothers would tend Naquel while I ran a few errands. Truly, to this day, I am deeply grateful for their presence in our lives and call them my attending angels.

Naquel continued to have seizures and developmental delays. At eighteen months we took her to a premiere children's hospital for a weeklong comprehensive neurological evaluation. I remember the cold, dreary December day when Lex and I were called into the doctor's office to go over the results. I was holding my breath and Lex's hand as the doctor began to speak. The doctor looked straight at us with expressionless eyes and a monotone voice, which I will never forget. He uttered a pronouncement that was both cold and unflinching. "Your daughter needs institutionalized care. The seizures have already done extensive damage. There is no hope for her brain to develop beyond that of an infant. She will probably die from her condition by the age of five – most likely from complications of pneumonia. I suggest that you institutionalize her as soon as you can."

If I hadn't already been holding my breath, his heartless delivery of such devastating news with such certainty and finality, would have knocked all the wind out of my lungs. His words hit me like a punch in the chest. I don't remember anything else that was said or what happened after that. I was in shock. How could this happen to my beautiful baby girl when I had done everything right?

We were staying at Lex's aunt and uncle's home about ten minutes away from the hospital. When we returned to Nancy and Bruce Coke's home that evening, they saw how absolutely devastated we were before we even spoke a word. They warmly embraced us. They took us - two broken-hearted parents - into their arms and wrapped us in their unconditional love. Their nurturance was deeply comforting. Without their support, we would have been inconsolable.

It was Christmastime and I don't remember ever feeling such numbness. My grief was completely overpowering. Nancy took me by the hand, piled me into her car and drove to a concert hall where we spent the evening watching a Christmas play. I was grateful for her warmth and love. Yet, the words, "Your daughter is going to die", kept looping in my head all night. Those words continued to torture me for months, no matter what else I was doing or who else I was with. Eventually, they became my new normal but the grief never abated.

We took Naquel home and continued to search for answers, refusing to believe the coldly delivered prognosis. We were blessed to have support, encouragement and help from our parents, relatives, neighbors, and friends. Some took Naquel for an evening, or an occasional weekend, so Lex and I could get a break from the 24/7 care our daughter required.

One evening when Naquel was two years old I was awakened by the familiar sounds of her having a seizure – only this time something was different. The seizure was followed by unusual crying. We took her to the hospital and learned, to our horror, that both of her femurs had fractured across from each other during the seizure. We had been tube feeding her for several weeks because she was unable to drink from a bottle or eat. She weighed only twelve pounds at this time.

The doctor looked at me and said, "Mrs. Harrison, your daughter is very ill. You will not physically be able to continue caring for her. Please find a high-level pediatric care facility for your daughter as soon as you can." I realized that the time had come for me to admit that I was not able to be the mother that I had envisioned. I wasn't able to provide her with the 24/7 medical care her complex condition demanded. Lex and I sadly agreed that it was time to find a facility to care for our beloved daughter.

Placing Naquel into someone else's care was both heartbreaking and a relief. We found a beautiful pediatric unit in a nursing home with skilled RN's who provided our child with high quality care. She made some progress with her weight, however, the seizures continued, as did the brain damage.

"Until you have a child with special needs you have no idea of the depth of your strength, tenacity, and resourcefulness." ~ Anonymous

FAMILY LIFE

⸺ ◆ ⸺

"There will be days when all you can do is breathe, and that's okay."

~ Fernando Sabino

Our second child, Lacy, was a few months old when we placed our precious firstborn, Naquel, in the high-level pediatric care facility. Lacy was a healthy, active baby who brought an immeasurable amount of joy to us and helped heal some of our heartache. She was a social butterfly. She was happy in the arms of whoever held her. But there would forever be that gaping hole in my heart for Naquel. I desperately longed to hold, kiss, and comfort her.

Kallie came twenty-eight months later and was exactly what we had hoped for, another sister for Lacy and one with a big bright smile that could make even the grumpiest person grin!

Our fourth and youngest child, and our only son, Chase, was born seven years after Kallie. His tenaciousness managed to cause havoc for his older sisters. He kept us on our toes and kept us young.

We raised our family in a medium sized suburban Idaho community. I was mostly a stay-at-home mom while Lex, a fourth-generation jeweler, worked more than full time in the 100-year old family retail jewelry business. Because Naquel lived just three hours from us, we were able to visit her weekly during those early years, even though she didn't show any recognition of who we were after the age of four.

We had many fabulous friends and some wonderful times during those years. We had our fair share of struggles, too, including a financial strain and marital stress that took a toll on our family. Lex was working very hard keeping the family jewelry business running. He was also in a position of service with our church, busy helping others. I sometimes felt overwhelmed by our financial pressures along with the frustration of trying to give our two teenage daughters the attention they needed while at the same time supervising our very active young son. I often felt that Lex was an absent parent and I was alone in raising the children. It was a difficult time for me filled with immense anxiety and oftentimes overwhelming depression.

I loved being involved in my children's school and sports endeavors. I served more than fifteen years on the PTA. I was a room mother, a substitute teacher, and a carpool driver.

I chauffeured the children to dance practice, recitals, soccer, baseball and football practices, and games. I drove them to their friends' homes and would have their friends over to our house. We had a trampoline in the backyard and had many parties and activities for the kids while they were growing up. I relished the chaos of these rambunctious gatherings because I knew where my children were and got to know who their friends were. When depression and anxiety were not on top of me, I enjoyed many wonderful experiences with my children while they were growing up.

As the girls turned into older teens, finances became more difficult. There were times when I retreated to the bathroom to sob behind a closed, locked door, hoping they couldn't hear me. Here I plead with the Lord to save us from financial disaster. I felt it was destroying me. Sometimes, the Lord answered my prayers with an unexpected windfall, but never with enough to turn things around permanently. I even got involved in the family jewelry business for a time and started a profitable branch. But it wasn't enough to sustain the store during the challenging economic conditions that existed.

As the unrelenting financial strain on our family continued, the stress became almost unbearable. At times, I felt like I was drowning. At other times, I was overcome with panic and thought I would suffocate. I literally couldn't breathe. Sometimes, I felt like a heavy, large black shroud covered me from head to toe in complete darkness and fear. It was so heavy that I couldn't move out from under it. The colors in my life seemed to fade into muted grays with some blacks and whites. A sense of joy eluded me no matter how hard I tried to capture even a little of it.

Despite intense inner suffering, I was careful not to burden anyone else with my distressed state. I made sure that when I was in public I had a happy face. I was friendly and helpful on the outside even though I was in deep pain on the inside. I tried very hard to pull it together at home. I wanted to maintain a positive front for Lex and Chase. By this time the girls had graduated from high school and moved away to college. Because Lex was going through his own ordeal with a waning family business and his other responsibilities, he couldn't hear me when I described to him the absolute hell that I was living in. I felt very alone. I couldn't find a way out of the bleak despair that had become my daily experience.

At the time, I thought it was the difficult situations that caused me so much mental and emotional distress. I didn't realize until much later that the overwhelming feelings of anxiety, along with the heavy depression that I couldn't seem to shake or get out from under, were due to a mental illness that had begun in childhood and had become more severe throughout the vicissitudes of adult life. Nor did I recognize that the suicidal ideation I would deal with off and on for over a decade was a symptom of serious mental illness.

"You will just never know what someone is dealing with behind closed doors. No matter how happy someone looks, how loud their laugh is, how big their smile is, there can still be a level of hurt that is indescribable. So be kind. Even when others are not. Choose to be kind." ~ Andrea Russett

CANCER

---◆---

"Sometimes real superheroes live in the hearts of small children
fighting big battles."

~ Anonymous

In March 2001, when Chase was twelve years old, the world caved in completely when he was diagnosed with Hodgkin Lymphoma. I was in shock. I was devastated. We began chemotherapy immediately. The previous six months I had been taking him to various doctors trying to find out why he was so pale, losing weight and was frequently sick.

One evening, I was able to get him into one of the busiest and most sought-after pediatricians in our area. He was also an acquaintance of ours. After reviewing Chase's test results, he gave us the devastating news – Chase had a large softball sized lump in his chest, lodged against his lung and esophagus. While Chase and I sat in the waiting room, Dr. Lloyd Jensen made calls to the same premier children's hospital that Naquel had been admitted to many years prior. He made arrangements for Chase to be admitted for surgery right away.

While waiting for Lex to come to the hospital I remember watching Chase stare into a large aquarium in the waiting room. He was quiet. I knew he was trying to comprehend what had just been explained to him by Dr. Jensen. He was trying to process what would happen to him within the next 48 hours. My heart was heavy but I was determined to be strong for my son. I said a silent prayer and immediately felt a comforting reassurance settle over my whole being. Somehow, I knew that Chase would be okay and he would survive this.

Once again, we stayed with Lex's aunt and uncle, Nancy and Bruce, who lived near the hospital where Chase was having the surgery. And once again they embraced us with their love and compassion. Their nurturing lifted us up and took us through an otherwise agonizing time. Even though Nancy and Bruce have both passed away, my love and gratitude for them is as deep today as it was during those times when they held our hands and tended our hearts as we anguished for our children. We spent as much time as possible with these dear loved ones before they passed. I was honored to be at Nancy's bedside with her children and grandchildren when she passed away.

One night, after one of Chase's chemo appointments I broke down and cried. I told Lex, "I thought that the pain we experienced from Naquel's illness would give us a free pass for our other children." Alas, there are no free passes. There are, however, many tender mercies that we come to recognize and cherish during our most challenging times.

By April, I knew something had to change. I simply couldn't continue living with this kind of financial pressure and at the same time support our son through cancer treatments. I asked Lex to give up the family business. It demanded too much of his time and energy. There were many days and weeks of discussions. I recognized that my mental health was declining and I needed more emotional support. It was very difficult telling Lex that I would move to Utah to be with my family for support and be closer to the hospital if our current situation didn't change.

This was a huge turning point for us. Lex agreed to shut down the business. We would move on. By August, after Chase's last chemo treatment and Lex's acceptance of a new position, Lex, Chase and I found ourselves packing up and moving to Baton Rouge Louisiana, leaving behind everything familiar, including friends and family. We were also leaving our daughters. Lacy had just moved to California. Kallie had already been living there for nearly a year. Though we were used to them not living at home, both girls had always been less than a day's drive away. Living in Louisiana would be different. The distance would prove to be greater than anything I could have anticipated.

As we pulled out of the driveway of our beautiful two story, colonial home for the last time, I was relieved to leave the financial pressure and painful memories behind and hopeful about a new beginning in Louisiana. But Chase was devastated.

He didn't complain, of course. But I knew. I had watched him say goodbye to his life-long friends over the past few weeks and I could see that it was breaking his heart to leave. His friends had been there for him through his ordeal with cancer. When he lost his hair from chemo, his friends from school, church, sports teams and the neighborhood came to our house to ask if it would be okay if they shaved their heads in support of Chase. Tears flowed as I watched these twelve-year old boys with their bald heads crowding around Chase in loving support.

This new chapter in our life was both terrifying and exciting. We were moving out of our comfort zones into the unknown. It was a relief to close down a business that had been financially drained due to the economic recession but it was also heartbreaking to close down the 102-year old family business. The jewelry business held Lex's family history and traditions. It was not easy to see it go.

"God didn't promise days without pain, laughter without sorrow, or sun without rain, but He did promise strength for the day, comfort for the tears, and light for the way." ~ Anonymous

THE DEEP SOUTH

———— ♦ ————

"I like stepping out of my comfort zone,
but this was more than I bargained for."
~ Kay Whiting Harrison

Lex accepted a position in Baton Rouge where he would manage a beautiful southern jewelry store. We were closing the door to one chapter of our lives and beginning a new chapter with just the right amount of trepidation and excitement. Chase wasn't quite out of the woods yet with his cancer. My depression and anxiety were somewhat under control but it was tenuous.

There were many things about our new home in Baton Rouge that were not to our liking - like the humidity, the heat, and the bugs. However, there were other things that made the move totally worthwhile, like the amazing, life-long friendships we made while there and how we pulled together as a family with prayer. Chase also grew and thrived during our time in

Louisiana. I often told him that I wanted to freeze him in time. He brought us and everyone around him great joy!

My premonition that Chase would survive proved true. Not only did he survive, he thrived over the next six years. He never once complained or allowed the cancer to drag him down. Instead, he embraced it. He decided that overcoming this challenge would be a defining aspect of who he would become. His courage and strength were so evident and inspiring. By the time he was fourteen-years old he was being asked to speak to audiences about his challenges and his positive attitude. He spoke about his cancer publicly for many years, inspiring others with his optimism and courage.

Unfortunately, my depression and anxiety continued to wax and wane during those three years even though I found a new therapist and med prescriber. The strain of living so far from Naquel, Lacy, Kallie, and other family members contributed to this. I continued to have suicidal ideation … but managed the best I could.

The years in the deep south were a mixture of highs and lows. We received many blessings and were dealt several agonizing blows. Our family enjoyed exciting new adventures mingled with bouts of homesickness from missing our daughters, relatives, friends and the familiar. My emotional rollercoaster of mental illness intensified during this period. These three years proved to be more challenging and trying than anything I could have anticipated.

"When you come to the end of your rope, tie a knot and hang on."

~ Eleanor Roosevelt

CALIFORNIA

———— ♦ ————

"I was the ultimate California girl, which is funny because I'm from Utah."

~ Kay Whiting Harrison

In 2004, Lex answered a call from a head-hunter offering him a position as a general manager for a store in Southern California. Lex hesitated. He had just accepted a promotion in his current position. However, he realized that this was an answer to our prayers and an opportunity for us to be closer to our daughters and other family members.

We made plans to move to California. Chase was in remission and had just started tenth grade. He loved his friends at the private school he was attending, but he was elated to be moving closer to his sisters, who were both now living in San Diego.

I immediately fell in love with our new community in California. I remembered my obsession with listening to the Beach Boys at the tender age of thirteen. I always longed to be a

"Cali Girl," and now I was one! All these years later, Lex and I were right where we needed to be!

I reconnected with my childhood friend, Claude Hicken, who had married June Moulton, a wonderful young woman from our hometown. They were living in nearby Coronado, an hour's drive away and we made plans to visit. We enjoyed getting to know June and the four of us hit it off. Claude took us on a tour of Coronado and all his properties and favorite classic car collections. He had become a very successful businessman. Still, he was just as down-to-earth, funny, and genuine as I remembered him. I teased him, "you can take the boy off the farm but you can't take the farm out of the boy."

We were happy settling into our new lives in California. For the first time in many years, we had three of our children near us. We missed seeing Naquel, who by now was living in Salmon, Idaho in the loving home of a wonderful professional caregiver, Dewey VanLeuven.

Dewey was a godsend to our family. She was a registered nurse who took Naquel into her home and became a loving surrogate mother to Naquel, tenderly caring for her for many years. We could not have found a better situation or person to care for our daughter! Although we still tried to visit her as often as possible, Naquel had no recognition or understanding of who we were due to the severe brain damage caused by her seizures.

Lex fell right into step in his new position and did what he loved most – managing a well-known jewelry store. It was an enormous relief not having the pressures of ownership. My career was a little slower to start. However, I was confident that I would eventually find my way. It was just a matter of time. I often turned to Claude for advice regarding business and difficult work situations because of our long-time friendship and my trust in him.

Unfortunately, it took me longer than I hoped. During those first few years when I wasn't able to pull my weight financially, I fell back into some anxiety and depression. I struggled trying to find a good therapist or psychologist to whom I could connect. During this time, I received several conflicting diagnoses. I wasn't sure if anyone was really listening to me. This was very frustrating.

Eventually, I was referred by an RN to a neurologist/psychiatrist who I developed a wonderful long-lasting relationship with. I will always be indebted to her. Working through the trials and errors of finding the best medication for me was made easier with her understanding and patience. The constant banging of my head on the career ceiling that led to my feelings of frustration and failure started to lighten up as we experimented and finally found the right medications. It was as if the skies started opening up for me professionally and personally.

My doctor helped me recognize some of the toxic relationships that I was in. She helped me figure out ways to remove myself from these relationships as best I could. With her help reducing the triggers and toxic relationships in my life, along with medication, I was able to pursue a life of skyrocketing business adventures. I made lifelong friends and experienced much success.

My twenty years of marketing background came in handy. Soon I was doing marketing for many businesses. Around the same time, other opportunities opened to me. I was elected chairwoman of a large chamber of commerce. I was a member of a community bank advisory board, and a hospice board before being recruited into the marketing department of a hospital system with two hospitals. My hospital marketing director, Brian Connors, and I had been business associates and friends before I was hired into his department. We still laugh about the year that he was my boss at work while at the same time I was his 'pseudo' boss at the chamber of commerce when he served as a board member.

I loved my career in the hospitals' marketing department more than any other career. Not only did the position open up great opportunities for me, I felt emotionally high due to the exciting nature of the work. Brian and I were always insync with ideas. We found much success and satisfaction within the department and working together. Brian was not only a great cheerleader for me and my successes but for everyone around him. Our goal as a marketing department was to develop a culture of trust within hospital staff and within the growing community. Brian and I were attending weekly and sometimes daily community, chamber, and hospital-related networking events. It was a flurry of activity, relationship building and extremely satisfying work.

"Sometimes I just look up, smile and say, I know that was you!

Thank You, God!" ~ Anonymous

SAYING GOODBYE

⸻ ◆ ⸻

"Time passes but not one day goes by that you are not here in my heart. The day you died was not just a day on the calendar, it was the day when my very existence changed forever."

~ Lorri Kitchen

On Sunday evening, Oct. 9, 2011, Dewey called us three times to let us know that Naquel was not doing well. We had received similar calls over the years regarding her health. However, this time we knew that it was very serious. Dewey encouraged us both to talk to her on the phone that day. Even though Naquel was never able to speak to us, she could hear us. We were painfully aware that her physical body would not understand but we were fully aware that her spirit would know that we were communicating our love for her.

While talking to her in the early morning hours of Monday, October 10, 2011, her vitals went up and then shortly later, she passed away. We left our home in Southern California to travel to Pocatello, Idaho to where Naquel was being transported from the hospital in Salmon, Idaho. We were so grateful that our daughter had lived so many years of her life being lovingly cared for by her surrogate mother and full-time RN, Dewey VanLeuven.

Our other three children, Lacy, Kallie and Chase arrived at the home of Lex's mother, who lived in Pocatello. We felt blessed to be together as a family for the first time in many years. I felt an incredible sense of love from being surrounded by all my children. We all felt a strong presence of Naquel with us. We reminisced late into the night about her and us as a family.

After purchasing a beautiful dress for Naquel's burial, Lex, Lacy, Kallie, her Auntie Anne, and I were able to dress her. This was one of the most tender and memorable moments we experienced as a family.

Both mine and Lex's extended families came together from various parts of the country, including my ninety-year-old mother. We were able to spend two days together. Lex and I had lived in Pocatello, Idaho for many years and many of our longtime friends from this area attended the visitation and the memorial at the cemetery. I will always cherish the memories of being with our beloved family and friends as we gathered during this bittersweet time. The most vivid and poignant of these memories was watching my husband, my son, my brother, my brothers-in-law and our sons-in-law carry Naquel's casket from the hearse to her final resting place.

On Friday, our family felt closer than ever as we said our goodbyes. Lex and I headed back home to California. Chase returned to college in Idaho. Kallie went back to Utah. Lacy and her husband Matt went home to San Diego. I remember thinking that we will once again pick up the pieces of our lives, find normalcy again and continue moving forward doing the best we can, always in deep gratitude for the time we had our precious Naquel in our lives.

"You have left my life, but you will never leave my heart.

Rest in peace, sweet Naquel."

~ Kay Whiting Harrison

"Irrespective of age, we mourn for those loved and lost.

Mourning is one of the deepest expressions of pure love." ~ Russell M Nelson

CHANGES

————— ◆ —————

"Some people believe holding on and hanging in there are signs of great strength. However, there are times when it takes much more strength to know when to let go and then do it." - Ann Landers

Within the third year, the administration asked me to start making visits to physician offices to promote the two hospitals I worked for in order to build trust and rapport with them. Eventually, I would leave the marketing department and move into the business development department. This was a bittersweet proposition for me. It increased my workload but it was very enjoyable work. I quickly became acquainted with most of the physicians on staff at the hospitals. I was also able to build relationships with many of the physicians in the surrounding communities.

Working as a physician relations manager, I and my counterpart, Nickol Logan, were the liaisons between the hospitals' administration departments and all of the area physicians. We spent most of our time with physicians, not only in their offices and in the hospitals, but also at social events, including lunches, dinners, and holiday parties. It was all about building rapport and trust. We worked to retain the business of the physicians already in our hospital community and we worked to bring new physicians and their business into our hospitals.

I loved this part of my career. Marketing is part of my 'DNA.' I enjoyed working with the physicians. Nickol worked with most of the surgeons and I worked with the general practitioners, cardiologists and cardiovascular surgeons. There were days when we had a lot of fun working together. Nickol was very bright and had worked in the medical field before I worked with her. One of my favorite opportunities as a physician relations manager was being invited to observe surgeries. I loved watching miracles take place on the operating table. I had come a long way from being the teenager who twice passed out in health class! The surgeries were fascinating!

When a new corporate director from the east coast took over all the physician relation manager teams, including ours, our workload and responsibilities increased substantially. The reporting requirements became intensified as our successful employment now hinged on meeting demanding quotas. We were pressed upon to bring in more and more physicians and surgeons to contract with our hospitals, while retaining the ones who already had hospital privileges.

The majority of the physicians I was assigned to were general practitioners. It was much more difficult to track the general practitioners than the surgeons or specialty doctors and as a result, much of my work with the general practitioners went unrecognized.

Nevertheless, I would spend long days meeting with physicians and cultivating their business. At the end of the workday, I was exhausted. I wanted nothing more than to go home and relax with Lex but often I needed to stay late to do the reporting, which sometimes took hours. It was one of these evenings and I was hopeful that I could finish up soon and go home and relax. When I looked up at the clock and saw that it was already 8 p.m. my body became wracked with anxiety. The desperation hit and I began to sob uncontrollably for about ten minutes. I started pleading with God. It was a simple prayer, "Please help me!" I'll never forget - within one minute of that prayer the phone rang. It was Nickol.

"Are you okay?" she asked. I started crying again. She told me to pack up my stuff and go home immediately. She promised to help me do the reports the next day and reassured me that she would help me get through this. I felt so grateful in that moment, both for her intervening phone call, and for the help she promised and later delivered.

Months later when Nickol told me she was resigning, I felt panic well up inside of me. I wasn't surprised Nickol decided to quit. My whole team had become increasingly dissatisfied with the east coast corporate demands. One by one, the other members of my team resigned. Unfortunately, at the time, I didn't believe resigning was an option for me. Being older than my counterparts, my perception was that I was too old to start over in another career or be able to find comparable work and pay. There was also a part of me that believed that resigning would be an admission of failure. This dilemma took quite a toll on my mental health.

My mind scrambled to imagine what it would be like working without Nickol. She had become a great friend, confidante, and a huge support to me. She was very smart and helped me through difficult work situations. I had confided in her about my anxieties that came from the increased job responsibilities. She was the one person who could truly understand the pressure I was under and someone who listened to me and validated me.

We had been working in two hospitals, both under one system, plus, a newly built sister hospital. In 2016 the administration from the new sister hospital requested their own dedicated physician relations manager. I decided to accept the offer which meant leaving the hospital system where I had been working for five years and going to work across town at the sister hospital. At the time, I was positive this was the right decision. I thought that it would be less stressful and a fresh start.

In my new position, I no longer worked with a dynamic team of friendly colleagues. Instead of a private office and being in control of my schedule, I found myself being pushed to the limits in a large co-op office with unrealistic amounts of work being piled on me at the hands of my east coast corporate director who was, to put it mildly, a bully. Not unlike the neighborhood bully I had dealt with growing up, this person had a passive-aggressive style and often made condescending remarks whenever I would try to negotiate. He would shut down negotiations by reminding me that I knew what I had signed up for.

I responded to my boss's aggressive style much the same way I did when I was bullied as a child. I automatically believed that I should be able to handle it and if I couldn't, then something was wrong with me. Instead of identifying and calling out mistreatment for what it was, I tried harder and harder to manage my emotional reactions and to find ways to cope with it. I also tried to avoid being on the receiving end of it by working harder to keep up with the relentless demands. When I felt despair over the situation, I would berate myself for taking it personally. I remember thinking that if I were only stronger and smarter that I wouldn't be affected by the bullying.

My mother had convinced me to see a counselor when I was a teenager for my anxiety and depression. I can't recall if that was particularly helpful, but I do remember thinking *back* then that something was wrong with *me* for not being able to cope. Even as a mature and successful businesswoman and active community member these types of thoughts and feelings persisted. At the time, I wasn't completely aware of this underlying self-blaming anxiety, but looking back, I realize now that I was re-experiencing the same feelings from childhood, but much worse. Unaware of all these dynamics at the time, I just kept trying harder to manage my emotions and working harder to keep up. The problem with this approach was the harder I worked, the further behind I fell and the more stressed out I became until I was utterly swimming in despair, anxious most of the time. Soon my body was running on adrenaline. It was all becoming too much to bear.

One late afternoon I remember driving to a chamber of commerce event and I became so overcome by the bleakness of my life that I started sobbing so hard I had to pull over to the side of the road. I asked God for help and relief. After a few minutes, I pulled myself together, cleaned up my face and got back on the road. I remember attending that event, with my usual smile and friendly chattering that effectively masked the emotional pain I was in.

"Beautiful fake smile. All it takes is a beautiful fake smile to hide an injured soul and they will never notice how broken you really are." ~ Robin Williams

INSIDE THE BLACK HOLE

———— ◆ ————

"Depression is like falling so deep down the rabbit hole you forget
what the sky looks like."

~ *Robin Brodsky Curtin*

I've always been diligent and compliant with my medications. Lex and I were both cognizant of when they needed to be adjusted. Lex often recognized it before I would. Along with other family members, Lex didn't always know how to deal with my mood swings or my depression. Even when he was trying to be gentle and helpful, sometimes his "help" came across as if he were saying to me, "Kay, your mental illness is showing." Neither of us realized at the time how certain statements triggered me into a downward spiral that could last hours, and sometimes days.

In between the "rough patches" I enjoyed many pleasant experiences with family, church, friends, community and work colleagues. It wasn't all bad. I experienced the joy of deep companionship with my husband and friends; the overwhelming sense of appreciation for the beautiful oceanscapes and scenery surrounding me; the fulfillment of completing projects and meetings that went beautifully; and the inner peace that followed worshiping with fellow believers. At times, I handled work and family pressures and stress magnificently. I was diligent in checking in with my doctor and managing my symptoms. Sometimes weeks and months went by without symptoms derailing me. There were even times when I was functioning so well that I couldn't imagine ever feeling the lows of my depression again.

Throughout most of our marriage, I thought my mood swings were a sign that I had something wrong with me - a character defect or weakness that I couldn't overcome.

I was easily triggered. The panicky "fight or flight" reaction surfaced so unexpectedly and so quickly, it frightened me. It seemed no matter how hard I tried to stop the reaction I couldn't control it. I felt angry that I had to live with this mental illness because I was only too well aware of the devastating impact it was having on my marriage and my family. I also felt guilty. At times, I believed that I was a very defective wife and mother.

I often felt alone. It was like living in a deep black hole under the ground while everyone else was living up in the sunlight - functioning well, experiencing success and happiness. I didn't like pulling Lex, or anyone else, down into that hole with me. So, I usually tried hard to find my own way out of the hole and through the thick dark sludge that held me down. I just couldn't get a good enough foothold to lift myself up out of the hole for very long before I found myself sinking back in again.

"Mental pain is less dramatic than physical pain, but it is more common and also harder to bear. The frequent attempt to conceal mental pain increases the burden: It is easier to say, "My tooth is aching' than to say, "My heart is broken." ~ C.S. Lewis

FOUR DAYS BEFORE
(Saturday, April 30, 2016)

———————— ◆ ————————

"You are not alone on this journey.

There are others walking this path beside you."

~ Anonymous

Lex never left my side!

Lex understood the stress I was under and he wanted to get me away from my home office for the day. I had mountains of work piling up and was falling further behind every day. Part of me knew he was right – it would be good for me to take a break. Yet another part of me insisted that I should spend my Saturday getting more work done so as not to fall even further behind.

Lex and I decided to drive to San Diego, to shop and find some quiet time. We had a favorite place that was isolated from the crowds and generally very peaceful. During the drive I stared out the window and past the scenery, completely lost in my thoughts about how I got here. How, on the surface, could I look like everything was okay and yet inside be in so much anguish and turmoil that I didn't even want to live? On the outside, I was well put-together, had a high-paying, prestigious position and was well respected in my community and my church. Yet, on the inside I was drowning in pain and sorrow.

Looking back now, I can see that I was in deep trouble. I didn't realize how my constant busyness and trying to keep up the outer appearance of 'holding it all together' was only hiding mountains of untold grief and unrelenting pain. From the outside, I looked like a model wife, mother, community member and professional. But on the inside, the pain and sorrow was swallowing me alive.

Staring out the car window, that last day of April, on our way to San Diego, I was so lost in my painful inner world that I didn't notice the massive green mountains or the beautiful blue waves in the ocean. Instead, I was painfully aware of only the mountainous grief and oceans of endless sorrow that I knew couldn't be contained anymore. I started thinking about how I could find some relief.

I thought back to the tragic loss of my firstborn child, Naquel. Not just her death at the age of 34, but the loss of all the ordinary milestones that mark a life; never having uttered one word or taken one step. I lost the opportunity of being a full-time mother and caregiver to her because her neurological disabilities were so severe that she required 24/7 professional medical care. Though we were blessed to find wonderful facilities and individuals to care for her, this loss was still difficult to bear. Added to this, was the profound sense of loss I experienced in the months after her birth as my lifelong dream of being the best mother to our child unraveled and eventually shattered despite all my best efforts, sincerest intentions, fervent prayers and strong faith and desire for my child's health and well-being. The harsh and stubborn realities dealt a death blow to that dream and it came unceremoniously crashing down around me.

My mind drifted to the gripping fear that I had experienced when Chase had been diagnosed with cancer at the tender young age of twelve. That fear, which had trickled through every cell and tissue of my body, was still palpable at times.

Lex asked me, "Are you ok?" I looked at him carefully and studied him before saying, "I'm fine," though I was anything but. I knew someplace inside that I deeply loved this man whom I had fallen in love with forty years ago, married and had four children with. Yet in that moment, alongside the love, I felt the enormous weight of what a burden I must be to him. My mental health had been up and down during our time together and I wondered how much more he could withstand.

We arrived in San Diego and wandered around the outdoor mall, ate lunch and made some purchases. I couldn't shake the heavy cloak of depression that was squeezing me or quiet the buzzing anxiety in my brain that kept screaming at me, "You should have stayed home and worked."

We drove to an area with spectacular views and found a quiet place to sit on a bench. We sat and I lowered my head and started to silently cry. Lex knew to leave me be. Even with Lex by my side I felt alone and distraught. I felt guilty for being a burden to him - for not being a better wife and mother. I remember thinking that I could have handled the many obstacles that were thrown in our path much better than I did. I thought I wasn't as appreciative of my blessings as I should be and I prayed silently for help to guide me through this impenetrable darkness that I was experiencing inside.

I felt a momentary and slight lightening of the heaviness surrounding me. I sensed a voice to my left, a clear, sweet and soft voice saying, "Mom, I'm here." I sat straight up and looked to my left. No one was there. I knew instantly and instinctively that no one would be there, and I also knew that the voice I heard was Naquel's. I heard my daughter's voice! My daughter who had never uttered a word during her entire 34 years on this earth had spoken to me! The gratitude and emotions that flooded through me in that moment were undeniable. This was the first time I ever heard my precious firstborn daughter speak even if it was inaudible to anyone else.

On the drive home, I told Lex what had happened. We agreed that it was a tender mercy and an incredible miracle for me. As we got closer to home, however, the unwelcome and unbidden heavy blanket of depression and intense sense of doom and anxiety began to devour me once again.

As soon as I walked in the door the pressure to get back to work washed over me like a sudden tsunami wave. I had no way to escape the pounding waves of pressure except to take something to help me sleep and go to bed, which is exactly what I did.

"My only relief was sleep. When I was asleep, I was not angry, I was not lonely, I was not sad, I felt nothing." ~ Kay Whiting Harrison

THREE DAYS BEFORE
(Sunday, May 1, 2016)

———— ♦ ————

"Mental illness can be terrifying because you feel like you've lost control of
your mind and nothing makes sense. It's like watching yourself on autopilot
and having little to no control." ~ **Anonymous**

The next morning, I struggled to get out of bed. I would have rather stayed asleep. Instead, I dragged myself to church and listened to a discussion with some of the women on the pressures of raising children and how noisy our lives can become. While most of the women were talking about their family and home lives being overwhelming and busy I spoke up and said something about financial and work pressure is different, but just as loud and distressing as the pressure of raising a family. I knew, as I heard myself speaking, that I was in deep trouble and would soon drown if something didn't change.

I remembered some recent phone calls with my then 93-year-old mother. I used to call her frequently while driving between the three hospitals I used to work at. I recall telling her on many occasions how exhausted I was but also reassuring her that I was okay. I missed my mom and wanted to spend more time with her but she lived in Utah and it never seemed like the right time to get away for a visit.

I silently wondered during these calls, "How long can I keep this up? Acting so smart and confident?" I felt like two different people. Smiling, happy, caring and outgoing on the outside while on the inside I could barely hold it together. I felt worried, overwhelmed and exhausted most of the time.

The incessant thoughts about not being able to keep up with the outer me kept swirling around in my head. From time to time, I would call my psychiatrist to get my medications adjusted. I stayed in close contact with her and trusted her. Being a medical doctor herself, she was aware of the work pressures that I was under. But my medications weren't taking the edge off like they used to and my inner and outer worlds were about to collide.

"There were days I longed to be the child wrapped once again in my mother's loving and protective arms." ~ Kay Whiting Harrison

TWO DAYS BEFORE
(Monday, May 2, 2016)

———— ◆ ————

"Nothing in this world can torment you as much as your own thoughts."

~ Val Rankin

I woke up on Monday morning feeling more than the usual amount of pressure and stress from the sheer volume of work that needed to be done. Not only that, but my job had become even more challenging when I no longer had an office from which to make private calls to the physicians and I had to go out the back doors of the hospital to an area by the dumpsters to get reception. I just wanted to stay in bed so I could sleep and escape my constant nightmare.

I had a meeting scheduled that morning with my on-site hospital director because I knew my workload was not sustainable. I carefully asked her if we could come to a mutual agreement on how to prioritize my workload. Instead of listening to my concerns, she told me to "figure it out."

I'm usually good at figuring things out, but not this time. This time I knew I couldn't figure it out. The churning critic in my head was screaming at me that I should be able to cope and manage. I had been through a lot worse, I thought. What was wrong with me? Why can't I keep it together?

"You know when you're in a bad dream and you're trying to run, punch, kick or scream, and your body just won't move? You open your mouth and nothing comes out. You feel frozen or in slow motion, and no matter how hard you try to fight it, nothing changes. That's how it feels to battle mental illness."

~ Evyenia

ONE DAY BEFORE
(Tuesday, May 3, 2016)

———— ◆ ————

"Before you judge my life, my past or my character, walk in my shoes, walk the path I have traveled, live my sorrow, my doubts, my fear, my pain and my laughter. Remember, everyone has a story. When you've lived my life then you can judge me." ~ Hemant Kumar

It was warm for early May. I drove home from work but I could barely breathe. I needed to get out of the house for a walk. I put my tennis shoes on and headed out the back gate to the path behind our home. It was a well-worn dirt trail, one that I had walked hundreds of times before. I knew this terrain like the back of my hand and yet somehow on this evening it was different. Everything was different.

I was walking in utter despair – desperately searching for something that I couldn't quite name or explain, let alone find. The tears welled up and spilled over as I silently cried and unsuccessfully willed away the profound and indescribable emotional pain. I began to panic when I saw a neighbor in the distance heading in my direction because I didn't want him to see me in this condition. Luckily, I had thrown on sunglasses and a hat so he didn't see the tears and emotion on my face. He asked how I was doing and I gave him a flat, "I'm fine" and kept walking.

After an hour of walking and trying to outrun the feelings of despair, I headed down a side dirt path off the main trail and found a secluded place in the ravine where I let the tears flow freely and sobbed. It was there that I pleaded with God one last time to please take this unbearable pain away from me. I asked for some peace so that I could carry on. I begged and pleaded to no avail. No answer came. No peace descended. I felt nothing. An even more profound feeling of despair besieged me. I had never felt so utterly alone, hopeless and helpless as I did in those moments in the ravine.

Looking back on this is heartbreaking because from where I stand now I can see clearly that God and the love surrounding me was present then. I just couldn't feel it or sense it at that time because having a mental illness, I learned, it can be like having a short circuit. As Jane Clayson Johnson explains in her beautiful book, 'Silent Souls Weeping', "The electricity is still there but the appliance isn't working because of a short in the wiring." Love and God were always there for me but the short circuit in my brain couldn't register that in those desperate dark hours.

I was no stranger to adversity and this certainly wasn't the first time I had felt pressure from the problems of life or financial strain, however, there was a different quality to the pain this time. Something about it wouldn't or couldn't let go of me. This was more intense and consuming than anything I had previously felt before.

The emotional pain I was feeling this time from the mental illness was incomparable and immovable when held next to the pain I had experienced with Naquel and Chase. I was conflicted because my work was deeply satisfying – serving as a liaison between physicians and administrations – and yet the pressure and tension was becoming more than I could bear. Yet, daily, I felt my life energy being sucked out of me due to mounting pressure coming from my corporate director. Short of quitting, which didn't seem like a viable option at the time, I couldn't seem to get a handle on things. I was flailing and failing.

I wasn't the only one having trouble communicating with the corporate director. Despite my best efforts to not let his remarks upset me, it took a toll on me each time he made an off-hand comment about my inability to manage my time or not being able to prioritize correctly. I continued to do my best to keep up with my workload, but each depreciating comment he made sent a familiar sting of humiliation through me.

I had talked to him about my frustration with the unrealistic amount of work and reports required. I asked for a prioritization of the tasks on my plate. He spoke to me as if he understood and he even made some encouraging comments. But in the end, he simply said, "Kay, you knew what you signed up for when you took this job." No changes were made to my workload. I felt utterly defeated and hopelessly overwhelmed. I desperately needed this burning pressure to go away.

I began thinking about how I was not only failing at work, but how I was failing everyone else in my life. My thinking was hijacked by depression and anxiety. It seemed that the harder I worked the less effective I became. I could no longer think straight, let alone objectively. I felt drained, depressed and panicky all at the same time. Sometimes the anxiety refused to let me sleep. At other times, the depression refused to let me get things done.

A vicious cycle had begun. I was alternating between feeling completely depleted and highly stressed. I felt out of control. The pressure was running me, overtaking me and overwhelming me. The harder I tried to get rid of it the bigger it seemed to get. Waves of overwhelming stress repeatedly crashed down on me until I couldn't breathe. The harder I tried to keep up the further behind I seemed to get. I felt trapped. Exhausted. Hopeless. I could not find my way out of the spin cycle.

Somehow, I managed to stand up and walk back home. I remember talking to Lex for over an hour about how anxious and overwhelmed I felt. He listened patiently but I knew he was weary of listening to me and he was frustrated because he didn't know how to help. I knew he was trying to understand but I remember feeling that the conversation was pointless, going in circles. When I retired for the evening, I let Lex think I was okay. I had not revealed to him the depth of my emotional pain or the state of utter hopelessness I was in. I didn't want to be a burden to him anymore. I had the thought of ending my life at this point, but I didn't have a plan. I was overwhelmed with exhaustion when I went to bed that night.

"I know what it's like to be afraid of my own mind."

~ Kay Whiting Harrison

WEDNESDAY, MAY 4, 2016

————— ◆ —————

"I don't think people understand how stressful it is to explain what's going on in your head when you don't even understand it yourself." ~ *Anonymous*

I decided that sleeping in was how I could escape the overwhelming pressure. Instead of getting up and going into the office, I decided that working from home would give me a couple extra hours of sleep (aka peace). When I finally got up and sat down at my desk, Lex was getting ready to head out to the gym and to run some errands. He kissed me goodbye.

Feeling a familiar sense of dread and pressure, I started to open my emails when suddenly my racing mind stopped cold and I heard my own voice reassuringly say, "You are done. Finished! You don't have to do this one more day!" I felt profound relief wash over me. An unusual sense of calm wrapped around me and I had an intense inner knowing that I would never again have to experience the unrelenting, maddening pressure and emotional pain that I had been unable to stop despite my most valiant efforts. Suddenly, it all just stopped. I knew it was time to make sure it never returned.

I quickly went to the bathroom and opened two bottles of prescription pills, including the last of some prescribed sleeping pills. I poured the entire contents into the palm of my hand. I looked at them briefly before I washed them down with a few sips of water. I decided I didn't want to risk waking up, so I also took the remaining pills in my bottle of antidepressants just to be sure to seal the deal. I remember saying out loud, "I am dying" and feeling a huge sense of relief. Contrary to what I've heard other suicide attempt survivors say, I did not have any regrets when I realized I was about to die.

I sat back down at my computer and opened a new Word Document. I wanted to leave a letter for my family. I wanted to apologize for taking my life and ask them for forgiveness. I told them how proud I was of each one of them and how much I loved them. I expressed my hope that one day they could understand and forgive me. The last thing I remember was explaining how unbearable this pain was to live with…

"I cry even harder, thinking of how it could have been, of how I thought it would be. For the first time, I want to give up, to die, because suddenly everything is too much and there is no solution in sight."

~ B.A. Paris, Behind Closed Doors

LEX
My Worst Fear

———— ◆ ————

I knew she had been struggling with her depression. I really thought I would be able to help her manage and get through this again - as I had many times before. The evening before her attempt, we sat at the kitchen table and Kay shared with me her feelings and her experience in the ravine behind our home that day. We talked for a very long time and I thought she was feeling better when she went to bed. Looking back, I now realize that she intentionally let me think that she was going to be okay.

Under the false and mistaken belief that Kay was doing better, I didn't worry about leaving her the next morning to go to the gym and then run some errands. I kissed her goodbye and told her I would be back in the afternoon. I usually work out for about an hour and a half but for some strange reason, on that day, after about an hour, I had a strong feeling that I should go home. I remember looking at the clock and thinking, well I can leave in half an hour when I finish my workout. A couple more minutes passed. I tried to brush off the strong feeling but couldn't. So, I cut my workout short, dressed and got in the car.

Forgetting the strong impression I had received at the gym, I considered quickly running my other errands first before heading home. But as I drove past the turn off to our house, I received the same strong urge I had felt at the gym. I immediately made a U-turn in the middle of the road and sped straight home. My heart was pounding and for some inexplicable reason I felt fear welling up inside me. The closer I got, the more anxious I became. I realized it must be Kay that I was worried about and that she was in some kind of trouble.

I ran into the house yelling her name. There was no response. I will never forget how loud the silence was. There are no words to describe the terrifying silence of hearing no response to my panicked calling out. It was deafening. I frantically ran through both levels of the house screaming her name over and over in a desperate attempt to find her. Nothing. Not a sound. I ran to the garage. Her car was there and she was not in it. I yelled again, "Kay! Where are you?"

I remembered Kay had talked about the ravine behind our house the night before and thought she must have gone back there. I ran into the back yard and was struggling to unlock the gate. My mind was racing, "How will I ever find her out there? Which path did she take? What if I go in the wrong direction?"

I somehow knew that time was of the essence. At that moment, I received another strong impression, "Do not go to the ravine, she is in the house. You must go back into the house NOW!"

I ran back inside and this time, instead of standing in the doorway of each room yelling her name, I did a thorough search of each room. Kay was in the office. I had missed seeing her before because her limp and lifeless body was lying hidden underneath the large desk. She had been sitting at the desk typing her last words and wishes to her family when the overdose of drugs hit her faster than she had anticipated. She passed out while still at the computer typing and slid out of the chair. She was lying crumpled up, almost completely hidden under the desk. Later, she told me that her plan was to take the pills, type the letter, print it out and go back to bed so that I would find her there.

I pulled her lifeless body out from underneath the desk and checked for breathing. Nothing. I checked for a pulse. Nothing. My greatest fear had become reality. I quickly called 911 and began doing CPR, thankful that I knew CPR. Because of my church responsibilities, I had been involved with the Boy Scouts of America for more than sixteen years. I had taught CPR and resuscitation to many scouts but never did I imagine that the one time I would need to use those skills would be to try to save the life of my wife.

I continued to do CPR until the paramedics arrived. I was not stopping! It seemed like an eternity before they arrived. Later I learned that the ambulance arrived within 6 to 8 minutes. When the paramedics arrived, I moved away from Kay and they started attending to her.

A flurry of activity began as they unpacked their supplies, pulled out IV bags, needles, medical devices and placed a portable oxygen mask over her face. As I watched this scene unfold, a paramedic motioned to me to take a look at the computer screen. I immediately recognized that it was Kay's suicide note but there was no time to read it. He then said to me, "Leave this just as it is. Do not do a thing to it and do not delete it. This will make the return trip home and the investigation much easier." I didn't understand what he meant at the time but came to find out later exactly what he meant.

Before long, they had lifted her onto the gurney, carried her down the stairs and into the ambulance. It all happened so fast. As they carried Kay past me, I will never forget the look that one of the paramedics gave me. Our eyes met, we looked at each other for a brief second. The look on his face was not one of hope, but of sorrow.

I planned to ride to the hospital in the ambulance with Kay but was surprised when they told me I couldn't. They told me I should follow them in my own car. I was irritated that they wouldn't let me stay by my wife's side, but didn't argue with them.

I drove behind the ambulance to the hospital. It was all a blur. Each moment felt like an eternity. I needed to know what condition she was in but had no way of knowing. When they carried her to the ambulance I wasn't even sure if she was breathing. I wondered how long it would be before I could see her or find out what her prognosis was. I kept going over all the good signs and bad signs in my mind. I remembered my eye contact with the paramedic and my heart sank. That was definitely not a good sign.

As I pulled into the parking lot of the hospital, I remembered all the times I had driven here before to visit Kay at work or to visit friends who were patients. It was hard to comprehend the reason why I was here this time. As I parked the car, I worried that Kay might not be alive by the time I got inside. I wanted to believe she was going to be okay but I was terrified that she would not be. I couldn't shake the look on that paramedic's face. I wondered what condition she would be in if she did live. She had not been breathing and had no pulse for who knows how long. My mind was shattered as I got out of the car and started running toward the doors.

I burst through the ER doors and told the receptionist that my wife had just been brought in by ambulance and stated that she was also an employee of the hospital. I looked around and realized that the large waiting room was full of people staring at me. I had not come in quietly or calmly. I took a breath and tried to speak as slowly as possible. I gave them my name, Kay's information and re-stated that she was an employee in upper management. I was hoping this would get their attention and move the process along faster.

The receptionist picked up a phone, turned away from me and spoke into it in a soft voice so I couldn't hear what she was saying. After hanging up, she pointed to a small private room off to the side and asked me to go wait in there. She said someone would be in soon to visit with me. My scrambled mind exploded in overwhelming fear. Why a private room? This had to be bad news. I felt defeated. I thought someone was going to come in there and tell me, "We're sorry, we've done all we can but your wife didn't make it." Why else would they have me go wait in a private room away from all the other people anxiously waiting to talk to a doctor about their loved one? I began to sweat and my breathing became labored.

I was numb as I obediently went and sat in the private room. It was later explained to me that the administration had told the receptionist to direct me to the private room because of Kay's employment status and need for confidentiality. After what seemed like an excruciating amount of time, a physician came into the room. He introduced himself, extended his hand and told me that Kay was alive.

Those words will forever echo in my mind - Kay is alive!

I thought my heart would burst out of my chest with overwhelming relief and joy. Before he took me back to the ER to see her, he tried to prepare me for what I could expect. He explained the seriousness of her condition. I pulled back the curtain to her ER bay, and what I saw matched his description exactly. There were four people working on her. There were multiple IV bags hanging and tubes leading into her body in multiple places. She was hooked up to a respirator that was breathing for her. At that moment I realized this machine was her lifeline.

I was offered a chair in the corner so I would be out of the way of everyone but could still observe what was happening. My eyes focused on the breathing machine and the sound it made as it breathed for her. After a short while, it dawned on me that I was breathing at the same pace and rhythm as the machine. Almost as if I was somehow, maybe subconsciously, trying to breathe for her, too.

While sitting there I had three visitors. The first was the hospital's CEO. She came to Kay's room as soon as she heard the news. She asked if there was anything she could do. She told me to contact her at any time for anything I might need. She also reassured me that HIPAA requirements, pertaining to a patient's privacy and confidentiality, would be strictly adhered to.

The second visitor was a hospital social worker. She wanted to know if I wanted to talk about what was going on and I said, "No, I'll be fine." I made some small talk and then she left.

A hospital security guard was the third person to come see me. He said that there was a police officer in the lobby who was waiting for me and that as soon as I felt emotionally up to it, the officer would follow me home and inspect the house. That is when I recalled what the paramedic said to me about not touching anything or deleting the suicide note on the computer. Of course, there would need to be an investigation.

I was informed that Kay was going to be moved from the ER into an ICU bed and the staff suggested that this would be a good time for me to go home with the waiting officer. They assured me that they would let me know which room she was in as soon as I returned to the hospital.

As the police car followed me back home, all the critical moments that had forever changed our lives came to mind. Then, suddenly it dawned on me that I was most likely under the suspicion of foul play at this moment. I felt more than a little upset by this. I was deeply offended. After what I had gone through to now be a possible suspect was just too much. As I turned the corner near our home, I saw another police car in the front of our house waiting for us. I wondered if the police had already done a background check on me or if they had listened to my 9-1-1 call.

The officers and I went into the house together. The officers read Kay's letter on the computer. Then they did a quick search of our home. Upon leaving, one of the officers extended his hand to me and said, "That's all. I'm sorry for the inconvenience during this very trying time. You won't be hearing from us again." He wished me well and thanked me for my cooperation. I thanked him and said that I knew he was just doing his job. He told me that this had been one of the easier situations of returning to a person's home to investigate a suicide attempt.

I can only imagine some of the tragic and terrible things that police officers must deal with on a regular basis. I came away from this experience with a much greater appreciation for the men and women in blue!

Much later I had an opportunity to read what Kay had written on that fateful day. From her words, you could tell that she was going to sign off soon and end her note - and her life. The memory of seeing her lying on the floor haunts me to this day. Sometimes, even now - years later - when she is lying next to me in bed, I want to reach over and touch her to make sure she is still breathing. Instead, I usually just stare at her intently to make sure I can see the rise and fall of her breathing. Then, I breathe my own sign of relief that she is here and she survived.

LEX
Managing Forward

———— ◆ ————

While in the ICU, Kay was intubated and carefully monitored as a respirator breathed for her. My two greatest concerns as I sat by her side were (1) how long would it take for the overdose of pills to filter through her body and (2) when would she be able to breathe on her own again, if ever? The sooner that both of these took place, the less risk of serious long-term impairment. I sat by her bed for hours becoming more and more acquainted than I ever thought possible with these machines that were keeping my wife alive.

I remember asking one of the nurses about the indicators. She was extremely kind as she explained to me that it could take quite some time before we would see any changes on the monitors. I continued to sit by Kay's side, watching and waiting for any sign of movements from Kay or sounds from the monitors that would indicate she was regaining consciousness. My thoughts now turned to our three children. I knew I needed to call them.

The thoughts about what had transpired the morning before, the current condition their mother was in and how to break the news to them, all looped repeatedly in my mind. I remembered the day, five years earlier, when Kay and I had to call each of our children and tell them that their older sister had passed. Now, I needed to make another call with devastating news - this time I would make the call alone. This time the call would be about their mother. The news I had to share would be shattering and yet there was still hope. I had to tell them. And we needed to gather all of our prayers, love and strength as a family to get through this.

I stepped out of the ICU room, paced back and forth in the hallway for several minutes as I contemplated the dreaded calls. I rehearsed what I would say over and over again in my mind. I wanted to remain calm and rational, keeping my own emotions in check. I wanted to give them accurate information about their mother. However, no amount of preparation can take the difficulty out of a call like this.

I called each one of the children, who were at that time, living in three different states - Utah, Idaho and Oregon. I calmly told them, while choking back tears, that their mom was in the hospital because of a suicide attempt. I told them she was doing better than expected at the moment but she was in serious condition. I told them of the events from the day before. All of them expressed shock and disbelief. Their reactions were of deep sorrow and concern for their mother and for me. They wanted to know what they could do. They wanted to drop everything and fly out immediately. I remember telling them that I didn't think it was urgent for them to come right away. I promised to stay continuously in touch with them and keep them updated on their mother's condition but until I knew more, they could hold off on their plans to come to California.

As promised, I stayed in close contact and gave regular updates as Kay's condition slowly but steadily continued to improve. Our daughter, Kallie, who is a registered nurse, was living in Oregon and she insisted on coming to support us. She wanted to be with us while Kay was in the hospital. We were so grateful for how she facilitated many helpful discussions with the medical team. She provided much needed support to her mother and me.

On the third day both indicators were beginning to move in the direction we had been hoping for. There was a sense of real excitement in the ICU as the physicians and nurses gathered around Kay's bed. Feeling confident that she could now breathe on her own, they began the process of taking her off life support. I watched her take her first breath without the aid of the machines. "She's back!" I thought. The tears spilled down my cheeks. A lump formed in my throat. Complete joy, happiness and gratitude filled my whole being. Little did I know what was in store for Kay, myself and our friends and family during the next several years.

It is difficult to put into words all the thoughts and feelings I experienced on that grim day of Kay's suicide attempt. I still experience minor post-traumatic stress every once in a while, as certain thoughts, ideas, and images flash to the forefront of my mind. Although I can't compare my P.T.S.D. to what others have suffered, I believe I have a better perspective and understanding of P.T.S.D. and have great empathy for those who suffer with it.

This has been one of the most challenging journeys of our marriage, and for our children. Because of this, we never underestimate how fortunate we are to be together and we never take each other for granted. We recognize the immense growth and positive changes that have resulted from this journey. We now take every opportunity to speak out, share our story, listen to others' stories, cry with and provide some hope to those who are going through similar challenges.

Our story doesn't end here. I am very cognizant of the fact that Kay has a mental illness and I continue to be mindfully aware of how I can support her continued recovery. Thankfully, she is managing her mental health and as a result, rarely has "bad" days. But we know that life happens. So, we both stay alert for triggers. Hopefully we will be successful in managing them and getting the support and help we need to do so. We now have a better understanding and knowledge of our own personal journey and how we can continue to be a strength and support for each other now and in the future.

AWAKENING

———— ◆ ————

"Take your time healing, as long as you want. Nobody else knows what you've
been through. How could they know how long it will take to heal you?"
— *Abertoli*

When I opened my eyes, I felt groggy, confused, and vaguely
surprised as it dawned on me that I was still alive. Or at least
I was being kept alive for the time being. I realized that the
excruciating pain I was feeling was from being intubated. Lex
was sitting by my side.

Everyone, except me, was relieved when I regained
consciousness. The reality that I had failed to end it all, was
almost too much as I realized the terror and anguish Lex and
my family had gone through while I had been unconscious and
intubated for the past day and a half.

A close friend of ours and clergyman of our faith community,
Tracy Ham, sat with Lex and comforted him while waiting and
praying for me to regain consciousness. Tracy had counseled

other members of the faith community and knew firsthand how faithful members of the flock struggled with mental and emotional health challenges. He was as deeply saddened as he was shocked in the recent turn of events.

"I never would have guessed that Kay, of all people, was struggling on the inside so much. I can't imagine how much pain she must have been in to try to take her own life," he lamented. Lex, feeling the sincerity and compassion of our friend, opened up and shared with him the struggles we had been through and how I had struggled with depression and anxiety since childhood. Lex also shared how I tried to keep my struggle to myself so as not to be a burden to anyone else.

Being a strong and competent woman who had lived through other major life tragedies had convinced me that I was resilient and could pull through this - until I couldn't. Until the day it was all too much and my thinking became too jumbled and too confused and I could see no way out - except death. It seemed so clear and logical to me at the time I made that fateful decision. My pain and suffering would be over and everyone's life would be better without me. It all added up. Little did I realize how distorted my thinking and emotions had become due to the unrelenting stress and pressure of my work situation mixed with depression and anxiety.

Despite my confidence in the hospital staff's ability to maintain confidentiality and the genuine kindness and respect shown to me, I couldn't help but feel the sting of embarrassment around the reason that I was now a patient in the very same hospital where just days before I had been privy to insider information - negotiating with doctors and administrators on high level priorities. It was incomprehensible to me how I could be a highly respected "mover and shaker" just a few days before and now I was lying here in a hospital bed, feeling ashamed and extremely disoriented.

Lex kept our friends updated on my condition. He carefully gave out only as much information as was needed. He fielded a barrage of questions, carefully dispensing enough information to satisfy the concerns without revealing the devastating event that led to my hospitalization. The words 'mental illness and suicide' were never mentioned.

The terms, 'possible heart attack' or 'stroke' were batted around by concerned friends.

Though Lex was a careful guardian, I recall some visitors still lurking outside my room waiting to visit me. I felt distraught about their presence. I wondered why they were there and if they knew what had happened. The instructions at the front desk were "No visitors allowed at this time."

Kallie was genuinely concerned about me and made sure the hospital was providing me with the best care possible. I was grateful she was there. At the same time, I sensed her frustration. I understood and accepted this as an expression of her love mingled with her own anguish and fear about what I had done and the pain that it caused her and the rest of the family.

I was in and out of a foggy awareness during my second and third day in ICU as my body tried to recover. I don't remember much other than the physical discomfort of intubation which was terrible and caused me to attempt to pull the tubes out of my throat. This resulted in staff putting me in physical restraints. They tied my arms down to the bed. This only added to my extreme discomfort.

After being moved from ICU into a hospital room I remember making a comment about being even further behind at work. Kallie brought me back to reality when she snapped, "Mother! You are not going to be working again for a very long time!" A tangible sense of relief washed over me. The unrelenting stress of workload pressure that had been bearing down on me suddenly lifted. Though my body was in physical anguish, my mind felt a bit lighter.

Because of my position as a physician relations manager I had frequently seen my neurologist/psychiatrist in a professional capacity outside of our sessions. She saw me behaving competently and confidently in those settings. This might be why my suicide attempt caught her off guard.

Three days after my attempt she visited me in the hospital. She asked, "Kay, why didn't you contact me before the depression and anxiety spiraled so far out of control?"

I paused to consider her question. When the thought of ending my life came to me that day, I didn't want to be stopped. Nothing and no one could have stopped me at that point. In my distressed mental state, this was the only answer - the only way out. That is why I didn't call her. I didn't say this. Instead, I said, "Because I knew you could change my meds or dosages but you couldn't change the pressure that I was under at work."

She looked at me solemnly and said in a gentle but firm voice, "Kay, if you had let me know how serious your inner suffering was I would have placed you on disability leave." Looking back now, I can see that if I had honestly confided in her about the full extent of my inner torment, she could have helped me and I may not have attempted to take my own life that fateful day.

Because I had attempted suicide, I was not allowed to return home. Instead, I was required to spend a minimum of 72 hours in a hospital psych unit for observation and assessment as soon as my physical condition stabilized. On Sunday, May 8th I was discharged from the hospital but didn't walk out the front door. Instead, I was wheeled out on a gurney, through the ER and past many employees that I knew from working with them. I felt humiliated and wanted to hide my head under the sheet. I was then transported by ambulance to a psychiatric hospital an hour away from our home.

"To that one soul reading this, I know you're tired. You're fed up. You're so close to breaking. But there is strength within you, even when you are weak. Keep fighting." ~ Anonymous

PSYCH UNIT

———— ◆ ————

"The souls that have seen the darkest days can shine the brightest light.

Keep going!"

~ Anonymous

It didn't feel real - and yet it was all too real - as I was being pushed on a gurney through the hallways of a psychiatric hospital. I was received by a team of workers, including a friendly case manager. She became my ally during my stay there. Lex had followed the ambulance and was with me during check in.

It was mandated by state law that a suicide attempt survivor be committed into a secure lock-down facility for a minimum of 72 hours. After that time, I would be assessed to see if I was ready for discharge. I was told that the more I participated with the groups and group therapies the faster I would heal and the sooner I would be able to go home. I planned to cooperate fully and be discharged as soon as possible.

Other than a slightly raw, sore throat and raspy voice from being intubated, I had no physical pain. I was still in emotional pain. However, I felt a wonderful sense of relief from the work pressure that had been taken away. My experience at this behavioral health hospital was a turning point for me. I remember the staff being genuinely kind and the atmosphere surprisingly pleasant.

Before being escorted to a semi-private room, I was wheeled past a large lounge area with chairs for groups, some game tables and an area to sit and watch a large screen television. The television volume was blaring. I paused to observe a diverse group of young men gathered, bantering and joking with each other, almost as if they were at a resort on vacation or on a break from school.

My room was large enough to hold two single beds, two cupboards, a sink and a mirror above it. There was an attached bathroom. My roommate was a middle-aged woman who was pleasant enough and quickly gave me her perspective on the hospital do's and don'ts as a gesture meant to enlighten me and create a shared bond. I listened to her as I carefully arranged my few personal items: a few articles of clothing, toothbrush, toothpaste, my glasses and contact case. Even my contact solution had to be locked away. I could only use it upon request. Being stripped of all my personal belongings, except the bare essentials, seemed to make sense in a place like this. I remember thinking, "Things are about to get very real." And they certainly did!

Every one of us who was there as a patient had been stripped, not just of our belongings, but of our roles, social status and any previous identities. We all stood on equal ground. No pretenses. We were each facing the realities and the raw emotions that had landed us in this psychiatric hospital. As much as I didn't want to be here, I knew I needed it and I knew I needed to face the truth and reality of what I had done.

Lex drove an hour each way to visit me every evening from 6 to 7 p.m. The first night we just held each other and cried. Other than the prayer and blessing he offered before he left, we didn't speak. No words were needed. Lex came every night. We prayed together before he left. I never wanted that hour to end and dreaded saying goodbye to him each night. I would walk him from my room, down the hall and into the area where the unit's large heavy locked doors kept me in and let him out. It was here that we hugged, cried and said our goodbyes.

One night, though, I said goodbye to him in the doorway of my room. I watched him walk down the long hallway and around the corner. I thought my heart would literally break from the sheer sorrow of watching him leave. I was overwhelmed. As I turned back into my room, I felt the crushing weight of remorse for all I had put him through. I laid on my bed and sobbed, grateful that my roommate was elsewhere so I could be alone with my raw emotions.

Feeling completely alone and totally broken, I continued sobbing. I caught my breath as I felt a warm presence at the foot of my bed and heard Naquel's voice say, "Mom, I'm here." It wasn't an audible voice but I heard it loud and clear. Naquel came to comfort me once again. I was profoundly grateful to her.

One of the patients I befriended was a young man in his early thirties named Tommy. He told me he managed a retail store. He was a self-admitted alcoholic and said he had voluntarily put himself in the hospital for one week of treatment. He seemed to have a different energy about him. He did not feel sorry for himself. He was forthright and honest. He was also everyone else's cheerleader. Something in me shifted when I talked to him and I resolved to be a friend to the other patients, like Tommy was.

Every day at 7 a.m., 12 noon and 5 p.m. we lined up in the hall and were escorted to the dining room for mealtime. On my second day, I was told I couldn't join the others in the dining room because of my status of attempted suicide. I protested that I had already been eating with the other patients and suggested that this was a mistake. The staff conceded and withdrew the orders and allowed me to dine with the others. I was relieved since socializing was what I needed each day.

On my second day, my roommate was discharged so my room became a private room. I was told I would have 24/7 supervision because the doctors felt I was still a danger to myself. I found this interesting but didn't protest. I didn't mind having the privacy of my own room. A staff member was assigned to me for 24/7 security. I actually enjoyed visiting with each person who was assigned to me. When I asked, they would tell me a little about their life and what brought them to their career in a behavioral health hospital.

On the third day, my social worker asked if I wanted to spend the rest of my stay with women my own age. I had observed this group of ladies over the past few days. They sat quietly together but exchanged very little conversation. "Heck no!" I said, maybe a bit too loudly. I wanted to continue participating in physical activities and games in the gym. I enjoyed associating with fellow patients who were also active and involved.

I attended group therapy sessions twice a day. I quickly learned the importance of telling my story about why I had been admitted. I did not feel judged by the others, who were all suffering from their own mental and emotional challenges. We were all on a journey to heal but we each had our own unique wounds. One young woman had admitted herself due to emotional trauma she experienced in her current relationship with a well-to-do attorney boyfriend. A young man in his twenties who was deaf, had been admitted for cutting and suicidal ideation. Some of these young men would have appeared very intimidating in the outside world, but I could see that they were just frightened and lonely. They were anything but tough in this environment. I learned that many of them came from extremely dysfunctional homes void of family nurturing. They were simply trying to cope and navigate the turbulence of young adulthood.

I befriended the young man who was deaf and asked him to teach me sign language. I gained his trust as I genuinely cared about him and requested to learn from him. One of the great lessons I learned is that everyone, regardless of where they are in their journey, needs to be acknowledged, loved and accepted. It was here that I was reminded again that although my mind was ill and broken at this particular time, I had an incredibly loving and supportive family waiting for me to come home. Many of these individuals did not.

Every day was highly structured. Meal-times, free-time, games and group therapy sessions all had designated times. Patients could choose to participate or not. I chose to stay active. I knew I was always being monitored and my release hinged on my participation. I found that my interaction with other patients was beneficial, therapeutic and healing.

I met with my assigned psychiatrist every other day. When I discovered that this behavioral hospital I had been admitted into was owned by the same corporation that I was employed by, I felt angry and bitter. I voiced my feelings to him regarding my director and the system. I was vocal about the mistreatment that contributed to my break down. The doctor listened. He didn't argue with the points I made. It felt good to be validated and heard.

However, at one point, he leaned toward me and said something that profoundly changed my entire perspective.

"Kay," he said gently, "we can physically remove you from the hospital that you work in, but what I worry about is 'can we get the hospital out of you?' Do you think you can do that?"

His words penetrated something deep within me. Suddenly, I knew with absolute certainty that it was up to me to heal and move forward. I didn't know how I would do it but I knew he was right. Somehow, I needed to let go of the relentless pressure and torment that I had been carrying inside of me.

Although I loved my career and wanted to continue, I knew I had to resign, not only physically, but mentally. I had to let go of the pressure and stress I had been under if I wanted to heal and recover. I finally realized that had I not been dealing with major depression and anxiety, I could have figured out how to effectively resolve the problems I was having at work instead of letting them cause me further damage. The importance of taking care of my mental health and making it a priority came through loud and clear. I committed fully to my healing that day.

I was hoping to be released on Friday but had to wait until the afternoon until the doctor could come and assess me. The person who was assigned to stay with me at all times on this particular day as my 'guard' was a cute young case manager. She stood about 5 feet tall and weighed about 100 pounds. After lunch we walked outside to the grassy courtyard to get some fresh air. An older man who had been admitted the day before walked toward us. He was still wearing his night clothes.

We began chatting. He asked, "Does it get easier being in here?" I answered, "The first 24 hours were the hardest for me, but it does get easier and it's important to get involved".

He became quiet and his eyes glazed over as if he were somewhere far away. Without warning, he punched me in the neck, hard enough that I fell backwards a bit. Thankfully, I was not injured. A security person intervened immediately, pushing him away from me and hustling me inside. Unfortunately, the gentleman who struck me without warning, had suddenly become psychotic and aggressive. It was recognized that he had been placed in the wrong wing of the hospital and was immediately taken to a more secure unit.

Later that afternoon when meeting with my doctor he told me that he had never - in all of his thirty plus years as the medical director - seen an incident occur such as this one. He lamented how unfortunate the incident was, offered apologies and expressed that I was the least likely person to have antagonized another patient.

Admittedly, the doctor's remorse over this incident worked to my advantage since he was the one who would determine if I would be discharged that day. I very much wanted to go home. I said, "Doctor, I have never been physically threatened like this before and it's obvious that the patient who did this should not have been admitted to this wing. I do understand the mistake. And I also feel very strongly that I'm ready to be released and I'm most certain that you will agree with me!" He discharged me that afternoon!

"Adversity is like a strong wind. It tears away from us all but the things that cannot be torn, so that we see ourselves as we really are." ~ Arthur Golden

STARTING OVER

"For what it's worth: It's never too late to be whoever you want to be. I hope you live a life you're proud of, and if you find that you're not, I hope you have the strength to start over."

~ F. Scott Fitzgerald

Upon discharge from the psychiatric hospital, it had been decided that I would spend the rest of the month of May resting and recovering in Park City, Utah with my daughter, Lacy and her family. It felt like an extended vacation. I slept in, took naps, went hiking and swimming and spent quality time with our three-year old granddaughter.

When I first arrived home from the hospital and before I headed to Utah, many loving and caring friends from our church wanted to bring meals and visit. Knowing they cared deeply about my well-being was reassuring but knowing that such visits would involve answering questions and talking about things I wasn't yet ready to talk about created anxiety. We decided to keep my suicide attempt confidential. Lex kept visitors at bay requesting they respect our need for privacy during this time. He explained that I had some memory loss and needed an extended time to recover before seeing visitors. To be sure, I had experienced some short-term memory loss due to the effects of the overdose, however, the larger reason we felt compelled to keep my mental illness and suicide attempt a secret was because of the stigma associated with it.

In addition to dealing with my mental illness and the after-effects of the attempt, I carried within me the private burden of shame. This was exhausting and emotionally difficult at exactly the time I needed support. I didn't see any other choice, at that time, but to hide the truth from others. I thought if people knew about my mental illness and my suicide attempt they would judge me, label me and look down on me. I thought my reputation at work, at church and in the community, would be ruined forever. I thought I would never again be trusted with any responsibilities. I thought others would lose respect for me if they knew. Given my propensity for being industrious and helpful, these thoughts were just too much to bear. I couldn't risk it.

At the urging of our children, we decided to move to Park City permanently and live with our daughter, Lacy and her family for an undetermined amount of time. My family knew me well. They knew if I stayed in California I would want to get right back into my old routines, which may have inhibited the healing work I needed to do. We now found ourselves in uncharted waters. None of us knew what to expect or how closely I would need to be monitored.

Though I was happy to be back in Utah, it wasn't easy to move away from the community in California that I had vowed to live in for the rest of my life. I loved the community and the people in a way that I had never experienced before. I had a genuine sense of belonging to both the land and the people. I loved that the ocean was only forty-five minutes away and there were many scenic hiking trails in the nearby mountains.

Before we moved to California I had done quite a bit of personal therapeutic work that enabled me to leave a lot of baggage from toxic relationships behind me. California had been a fresh start – like a fresh breath of air. Some of the happiest moments of my life happened in California. It was in California that I met some of my most cherished friends from the community and from our church.

I had felt euphoric attending frequent chamber of commerce meetings, networking and community events. These meetings were always packed with interesting people and lively conversations about a variety of topics. I was honored to be in a leadership role. I was well respected and felt a deep commitment to this community and wanted to continue contributing to it. The natural adrenaline rush from some of these events would often last for several days. Before my attempt, I could never have imagined myself voluntarily leaving this lifestyle, this landscape, my friends, or this community.

"You left a forever-California imprint on my heart. It would take pages to list your names. Just know, you're on it." ~ Kay Whiting Harrison

THERAPY

———— ◆ ————

"Sometimes you need to hang on to someone else's hope. Someone else's peace and sanity while yours is under siege. Strength, peace, courage with them all come and go when we face trials. Borrow someone else's light until your light can shine brightly once again." ~ Anonymous

As part of my discharge plan from the psychiatric hospital it was required that an appointment be set up with a therapist in Park City to ensure continued care. At the luck of the draw, I was linked to Bobbi Fosburg, a licensed clinical social worker, who turned out to be an incredible therapist, an amazing person, a godsend to me and a catalyst in my recovery.

Bobbi showed me the value of facing and working through the most difficult mental challenges and resulting painful emotions which I had been resisting. In all fairness, before working with her I didn't know how to deal with much of this emotionally. For four months, we worked hard to uncover my demons and put them to rest. It felt like my life was being saved and there was a tiny glimmer of hope starting to emerge, that is until five months into the therapeutic process when I had to return to California to see my psychiatrist and renew my prescription.

The day before my flight, I learned of some rumors going around that the reason for my hospitalization had been a drug overdose. There were whisperings that I was a drug addict. It was true that an intentional drug overdose was the reason I had been hospitalized but it was not true that I was a drug addict. These rumors completely devastated me. I cut my trip short and didn't visit with many of the friends I had planned to see. I felt shocked and broken. It seemed as if all the good that I had accomplished in the community over the last twelve years didn't count for anything. In fact, it had all been quickly replaced by an ugly label, "drug addict." This resulted in a deepening depression and anxiety that I struggled with for the next year. I stayed in therapy with Bobbi in Park City, who I can truly say, "helped save my life."

For the next year, she treated me for Post-Traumatic Stress Disorder (PTSD). I learned that PTSD can affect anyone and it can show up in different ways. I had previously thought that PTSD only affected veterans of war who experienced horrible atrocities. I learned that any event or experience that overwhelms a person's capacity to cope can leave a traumatic imprint on the person. This includes accidents, loss, abuse and/or toxic relationships. Bobbi used E.M.D.R. (Eye Movement Desensitization and Reprocessing) to help me process the emotional impact of past traumas. I felt as if there had been a deep rut, crater or crack in my 'being' that started with childhood bullying. Another toxic relationship during my adulthood had deepened the groove. Then the rumors of being an addict cracked that wound wide open. It was excruciating. Each time I was triggered, that rut would grow a little deeper and that wound would be exposed again, until I did EMDR.

I found EMDR to be completely therapeutic, releasing me from the trauma I experienced. After the emotional charge from the trauma was released, the next step to healing was my own decision to forgive those who had hurt me. I knew that this was an important step for my own healing and peace of mind. It came slowly. Through much prayer and the passage of time, I was eventually able to forgive those who hurt me and let go of the pain associated with those relationships.

"Hope isn't the alleviation of fearful risk, or the sidelining of anxiety.
It's the choice to see beyond the current circumstances
to something better despite the presence of those feelings."
~ Ron Carucci, Organizational Change Consultant

FORGIVENESS

———— ◆ ————

"Forgiveness does not always mean reconciliation.
It is possible to forgive and still walk away." ~ *Morgan*

I have at times been outspoken regarding forgiveness. Forgiving someone doesn't mean condoning what a person did that harmed you. Nor does it mean you must resume a relationship with them. We need to preserve and protect ourselves from toxic relationships whenever possible. We often don't recognize toxic relationships for what they are while we are in the middle of them. However, as we start to step away and look at them objectively, we start to see the toxic dynamic. Then we can take some space and find some relief. Often as we let go of toxic relationships, we experience a tremendous peace that we didn't even know was possible before we let go.

It was difficult to acknowledge the toxic relationships I've had during my lifetime. I now realize I wasted too much precious time with these individuals. I tried very hard to make the other person happy, hoping they would approve or acknowledge my talents or accomplishments, all to no avail. In actuality, I learned that it was not me who was flawed in the relationship but the other way around. Toxic people tend to be insecure and their insecurity is masked as a need to be in control or have the upper hand over others.

In one particular relationship, I completely stepped away and removed myself from this person for several years. I was astonished by the emotional freedom I found. No longer did I constantly hear, "You can't do that" or "You're not smart enough". Instead, I found a community of very kind, intelligent people from all walks of life who were not only great examples and mentors in the community but also in the business world where I learned to not only follow their example but to lead by example.

It's heartening to know that we can learn, grow and change from these types of negative experiences. Recently, someone I cared about did something that deeply hurt my feelings. It was no doubt an intentional attempt to hurt me. And it did. I spent a few days fretting but then remembered to use the tools I learned in therapy. After meditating and praying about it, I recognized what was happening. I remembered that I had the power to do something about it. I did not want to get stuck in these toxic feelings. I received an answer which was very clear and powerful for me, "Take back your energy, your power and time. Don't give it away to those who don't value you." I immediately was able to do so and this gave me immediate relief from all the negative feelings I had been experiencing around this situation.

"If you knew how hard it was and how long it took to rebuild my little universe of peace and happiness then you would understand why I'm so picky about who I allow in my life." ~ Anonymous

COMING OUT

—————— ◆ ——————

"I'm a success today because I had a friend who believed in me and I didn't
have the heart to let him down." ~ Abraham Lincoln

My son, Chase, and I have always had a close bond. When
he was young, we spent a good amount of time together while
fighting his cancer. As much as I tried to hide my depression and
anxiety, and I never openly discussed it with him, he knew there
were challenges. As he got older, neither he nor my daughters,
ever held my mental illness or the suicide attempt against me.
My children, Lacy, Kallie, and Chase, have all, without question,
always supported and loved me unconditionally.

Even on that almost fateful day of my suicide attempt in 2016,
Chase had a firm conviction that I would not only survive but
that I would write a book about my experiences to help others. It
is he who has pushed and encouraged me to share my story and
write this book, in full faith that my story would have the power
to help others who are also struggling. I, on the other hand, was

terrified of openly admitting that I had a mental illness and had attempted to end my life.

In some ways, it was easier being in Utah and making new friends who knew nothing about me. A fresh start. Despite Chase's certainty of me sharing my story publicly, I couldn't imagine, in my wildest dreams, that I would openly share my experiences with mental illness, especially my suicide attempt, with anyone.

Then one day in the winter of 2016 I was attending a church meeting. A couple spoke about their son who had suffered with mental illness his entire adult life. It was heart wrenching to hear about how much they had suffered. I didn't know this couple well but after the meeting I walked up to them and thanked them. I put my arms around them and started to cry. Finally, I had met someone whom I could relate to and they to me. I felt the weight of stigma and shame beginning to lift from my shoulders.

I became fast friends with Lana Youngberg, the mother who opened her heart to me. She suggested I attend an upcoming event that a local nonprofit was hosting. Lana and Rob were co-founders of CONNECT Summit County, in Park City, a local mental health advocacy organization, along with another couple, Ed and Lynne Rutan. I learned of Rutan's son, who had a mental illness and learned about their journey with him. As I became more involved with CONNECT Summit County, and with people who were talking openly about mental illness and how it impacted their lives, I couldn't get enough. Suddenly, I wasn't alone. I surprised myself as I heard myself - face to face - talking openly about my own mental illness and suicide attempt.

It was such a relief to be among like-minded people who not only accepted me without judgment but who also warmly welcomed me into their community of advocates fighting to destigmatize mental illness and help those suffering and their families. It gave me a safe place to share and to give and receive support. It felt wonderful.

I began volunteering for every event I could. I wanted to get to know as many people as possible and learn about their stories. I discovered that I was a bit of an anomaly because most of the volunteers and board members were parents and spouses of loved ones with mental illness whereas I was a person with a mental illness. I was the suicide attempt survivor.

Here were people who not only accepted me after I told my story, they actually appreciated me for telling my story. I think they were amazed at my courage in being so open. I was amazed that I was being so open.

In April 2019, Lynne called me. She told me that the Park Record newspaper was looking for someone to interview for a piece on mental illness. She asked if I would be willing to go public with my story and do the interview. I heard myself respond instantly, "Yes."

I am still astonished at the whirlwind of my 'coming out.' I did the interview and shared openly about my struggles with mental illness and my suicide attempt. The reporter took my picture. I remembered what Chase had told me and knew it was the right thing to do. It was important to share stories like mine. They might help someone else.

The next day I began feeling a little apprehensive. Sure, I had openly talked about my experience to many different people, mostly one on one, but this was different. This was going public. This would be in print. I emailed the reporter and asked if she could bury the article somewhere in the middle of the newspaper. She told me no, the editor thought it was too important and wanted it on the front page. I braced myself.

Lynne called me early the next morning and asked if I had seen the paper. I said, 'Not yet." She handed the phone to her husband, Ed. He emotionally told me how grateful he was for my courage in talking about my mental illness and suicide attempt. My head was whirling when Lynne knocked on my door, handed me the newspaper and hugged me tightly.

When several of my family members learned about the article, they expressed concerns about the possible backlash I might experience. They were genuinely worried that it might be a setback for me and were afraid that my mental health might not be able to withstand a lot of negativity directed at me because I had publicly disclosed personal information about my illness and my attempt. I felt confident that I could withstand any negative reactions because I was not alone. I had developed supportive friendships with those I met and worked with through the advocacy organization.

The following day the newspaper reporter started receiving emails from individuals requesting permission to contact me. People and organizations were thanking me for being open and honest and sharing what I had for so long tried to hide. The best way to describe this unexpected transformation was a 'mental illness coming out' – no more silence or hiding the awful rollercoaster of mental illness anymore.

I've been speaking out about my experiences with mental illness and my suicide attempt ever since. I'm still quite private about some of my experiences and rather selective about who I share intimate details with. It's not always comfortable to talk about these things but I feel very compelled to do so and it is getting easier.

"The experience I have had is that once you start talking about [experiencing a mental health struggle], you realize that actually you're part of quite a big club." ~ Prince Harry

SPEAKING OUT

————— ◆ —————

"I'm thinking that I'm brave enough now to step out of my past and into the new story I'm ready to write." ~ Kay Whiting Harrison

Ironically, moving away from California gave me a measure of peace. I felt reassured that the history of my mental illness and my suicide attempt would be quietly left behind and no one in my new community would ever have to know. I never imagined I would voluntarily speak out about it in my new community. Of course, I recognize that my privacy was a necessary part of my healing journey at that time and I am grateful for the way we handled it. It just never occurred to me that speaking out would also be a part of my healing journey.

As I began speaking out in my new community, I began to think about the dear friends we left behind in California who didn't know what happened. They had many unanswered questions - like why had I been hospitalized and why did we move away so abruptly? At the time, we thought this was the best way forward. I didn't realize that eventually I would feel compelled to disclose the full story to these beloved friends and that this was yet another part of my healing journey. It's not that we disappeared, but we didn't disclose the full reason for our sudden move.

On June 29, 2016, the day before we drove away from our California home to move to Utah, we invited all our best friends over for a pizza party and a chance to properly say goodbye. They generously helped us with lifting the last remaining heavy items into our moving truck. With tears and hugs we all said our goodbyes. We dearly loved this wonderful group of friends who gathered to see us off. They accepted our explanation of needing to be closer to our children and relatives. This was partially true, of course.

In 2018, shortly after I had started speaking openly locally about my mental illness and suicide attempt, I began to formulate an email to my friends and close associates in California. I struggled to find the right words. I went back and forth for weeks, vacillating between my desire to be open and share the deeper reasons for our sudden move and the fear of opening the door to potential criticism and possibly the loss of some friendships. Stigma alone is a powerful reason for not disclosing this kind of information.

Still, I felt compelled to do so. My mind was swirling with questions, such as, "Am I sure I want to do this? What if they reject me after I am honest with them? Will my heart break? Will

I be able to accept their reactions and any possible consequences that might result from this disclosure?"

Eventually, I resolved to send the email and explain the answers to all the unanswered questions. Feeling inspired to do so out of an abiding love for these dear friends, I hit "send."

In a very short time, I began getting replies to my email. Friends were thanking me for telling them the truth and appreciating my courage in doing so. They complimented me for coming forward to talk about something that needed to be talked about but that too many people resisted talking about. My fears continued to dissipate as I read each heartfelt email from all our closest friends. Truly, a weight had been lifted.

I had personally called Claude to share what happened around the same time I sent the "coming out" email to my other friends. He reacted the same way most everyone else reacted. He said, "I would never have thought that you struggled with mental illness. What can I do to support you?" And he did what he usually did - listened to me share my story with love and non-judgment.

Tracy Ham, who had sat with Lex that first night in the hospital, was one of the few people who knew the whole story about why we moved away and had been a huge support to us ever since. He contacted me after receiving my email. He asked if I would be willing to come to California in the near future and speak to his congregation and my previous congregation in an evening meeting.

Tracy had told me before we moved away, "Kay, if you ever get to the point where you feel comfortable speaking about your mental illness and suicide attempt, I can see it helping a lot of people. Even if your story only saves one life, Kay, it will be well worth what you've gone through." The moment he spoke those words something inside me knew that one day I would eventually step out of my comfort zone that favored privacy and start speaking openly about these excruciating events. I just didn't know it would be so soon.

We were scheduled to speak in California on May 19, 2019. Lex and I spent months working on our presentation. Throughout my career I had regularly presented to large audiences. With the exception of a normal amount of nerves, I mostly felt confident and competent speaking.

I called Claude and asked if he and June would attend the fireside meeting where we would be speaking. Although I knew there would be many other friends in attendance, I knew it would be a great comfort having Claude and June's presence and support. To this day, that presentation to over 300 in attendance, half being good friends and acquaintances, was the most terrifying experience of my life! After the hour-long presentation, Lex and I answered questions for over forty-five minutes. I was overwhelmed with the acceptance and love we received from the audience.

Several months later, June called and asked us if we would speak at their church for their congregation in California and we accepted. Again, we experienced a warm welcome and acceptance as we shared our experiences hoping we could help someone else who might be struggling in silence. We answered many questions. We emphasized that we are not professionals or clinicians. Our motivation for speaking out is because we have lived the experience of mental illness and have a strong desire to help prevent others from attempting suicide.

Lex and I spent the weekend with Claude and June going to places in San Diego and Coronado that we had never been to before. Claude spoke openly about some health problems that he was experiencing and would need surgery for. He was confident in the outcome and appreciated being able to share time with us.

"True friends are medicine for a wounded heart,
and vitamins for a hopeful soul." ~ Steve Maraboli

CONTINUING THIS JOURNEY

———— ◆ ————

"The more education I sought, the more strength I gained."

~ Kay Whiting Harrison

In 2018 I attended a presentation about a method for helping people with serious mental illness called LEAP (Listen - Empathize - Agree - Partner). I went with the Rutans, along with several other mental health advocates in Park City. It was held at the University of Utah in Salt Lake City. I was curious about the method, the LEAP Foundation and the founder of the method, Dr. Xavier Amador. Many in attendance were mental health professionals and family members of individuals who have a serious mental illness that included Anosognosia, which is an inability to recognize their own clinically diagnosable symptoms. I learned that approximately fifty percent of people with schizophrenia and bipolar have Anosognosia.

There was a second day of training for those of us who were interested in becoming certified to teach this method. We were invited to participate in this all-day training in Park City. I was on board. The training was led by Dr. Amador. A dinner followed, hosted in his honor. His personal story is fascinating. I learned how he developed the LEAP Method in an effort to help his own brother who had been diagnosed with Schizophrenia. Dr. Amador is an internationally renowned clinical forensic psychologist and a leader in his field. He has authored several books and been featured on news programs. He has held speaking tours about his work on his high-profile forensic cases. But his heart's work is in helping family members who have loved ones with serious mental illnesses. His goal is to teach and train the LEAP Method to as many as possible.

I was very impressed with Xavier and took every opportunity to become better acquainted with him. I wanted to learn all I could. Through the Rutans' hospitality, Lex and I began skiing with them and Xavier. We discovered that we all shared the same passion for skiing. With some encouragement from us, Xavier moved to Park City part-time. We now spend a good part of the winter skiing together. Lex and I appreciate the bits of wisdom Xavier dispenses on the chair lifts and when we share dinners together. We've also been sailing with him on a week-long adventure out of Long Island, New York. Oh, the things we learned!

After becoming certified L.E.A.P instructors, Lynne Rutan, Carol Labrizzi and I began teaching L.E.A.P. classes to family members in our community. Before COVID, we taught in person and during COVID, we taught virtual classes. Although I have not experienced Anosognosia, as I was aware of my symptoms, I do introduce myself as a suicide attempt survivor and a person who has the lived experience of struggling over a lifetime with clinical depression and anxiety. I believe that anyone can be helped by practicing these skills. I also practice them when I am talking to individuals in the community.

Not long after the newspaper article in 2019 I was asked by the behavioral health clinic where my therapist worked if I would be interested in certifying as a Peer Support Specialist. I did not fully comprehend what this meant but decided to do it. I also signed up for other training courses and certifications in mental health. At first I thought I was doing these training sessions to help myself by increasing my own knowledge. Later I realized that there may be a bigger reason I've been pursuing multiple certifications in mental health, including Suicide Intervention, Youth Mental Health First Aid, QPR, (Question, Persuade, Refer). That bigger reason is to help others, too.

"I want to inspire people. I want someone to look at me and say, because of you, I didn't give up." ~ Anonymous

CLAUDE

———— ✦ ————

"Your friendship has helped me grow, kept me grounded, lifted my spirit, and brightened my life." ~ Kay Whiting Harrison

During the time I was 'coming out' publicly, I was also chairing and working on our high school class reunion. I immediately asked Claude if he would be on my committee. I invited him to be on the committee, not just for his expertise but primarily so he could share his zest for life, his great sense of humor and keep all of us feeling lighter and entertained. We spent two years in close contact on the planning committee, texting, calling and emailing. His out of the box thinking always made it into our plans.

On November 13, 2020, I received word that Claude had been hospitalized for leukemia and had died within days. The disease had caused extremely thin blood and some had seeped into his brain. I was crushed by the unexpected loss. I had lost my firstborn child, my parents, grandparents and other loved ones but this was different. I had seen their deaths coming from either old age or a terminal condition. Claude's death was so unexpected that it sent me reeling.

I felt the loss of a long-time, trusted friend whose support I cherished. From childhood he had made a tremendous difference in my life. This was a dear friend who was so funny, so happy, and so full of life one day and suddenly gone the next.

The grief I experienced at Claude's death was like no other grief I had ever felt. I felt myself spiraling downward but not into the same void of depression that I had lived with for so long. It had a different texture and feel to it. I called Bobbi and we talked about a process to help me manage my grief. It took months before I could speak about him without descending into a pool of tears. I talked to June as often as possible and we would laugh and cry together remembering so many memories of Claude.

One sleepless night, I woke up and sat in the dark at the top of the stairs and asked God if He would just sit with me while I grieved this great loss. Within an hour, I felt a sense of relief wash over me and ever since the grief has turned into fond memories. I recently heard a saying about grief that says, *"Grief is love with nowhere to go." William Spense.* To this day, I stay in close touch with June because of my love for both her and for Claude.

"The darker the night the brighter the stars. The deeper the grief, the closer is God!" ~ Fyodor Dostoevsky

FINDING HOPE AGAIN

---◆---

"There is hope, even when your brain tells you there isn't" ~ John Green

I have received hope from several other authors who have shared their own stories and spiritual perspectives on mental illness. Here is one of my favorites:

"The words suicide and hope sit together oddly on the page. Suicide is, after all, what happens when someone loses hope; it is the ultimate act of despair. But there is always hope," says Jane Clayson Johnson in her book, 'Silent Souls Weeping'.

This quote resonates with me because I can see how my brain was processing nothing but guilt, complete failure, exhaustion, and wanting out of the excruciating pain. Love works to heal because it is hopeful. It illuminates the possibility of a joyful future.

Everyone who suffers from a severe mental illness is on their own path of hope. For me, receiving complete and unconditional love from my family and the affirmations of God's love filled my soul with hope and peace once again.

"Blessed is the man that trusteth in the Lord, and whose hope the Lord is."

~ Jeremiah 17:7

My Journey in Finding Hope Again

Faith in God

Family

Prayer

Therapy

Meditation

Healthy Diet

Exercise

Time for self

"I sought the Lord, and he heard me, and delivered me from all my fears."

~ Psalms 34:4

CONCLUSION

———— ◆ ————

"And one day she realized that she was fierce, and strong, and full of fire, and that not even she could hold herself back because her passion burned brighter than her fears." ~ Anonymous

I've come a long way since that day I decided to end my life in 2016. Looking back, I would not want to go through that experience again but I also wouldn't trade it either. The insights and growth I've experienced as a result of my attempt and recovery have fortified me and prepared me to help others. I believe I am here to help others struggling with mental illness and to help break down the stigma that prevents them from reaching out for help. I firmly believed that I wanted to die, to end my pain. I didn't think there was any hope for me to get better. I was wrong. I want others who are considering this option to reconsider and believe me because I have been there and I know I was mistaken. Suicide was not the only option.

Toward the end of writing this book, I surprised myself when the word "gratitude" came into my mind. I never expected to feel grateful for the many struggles and losses I experienced throughout my life, including my suicide attempt and my struggles with mental illness. However, today I can honestly say with complete certainty that I am deeply grateful for this journey I've been on and I'm grateful that I survived and am alive to write this book and share my story with you.

Telling my story has been a bittersweet experience. If I'm honest, it's been extremely difficult to put this experience into words and relook at it all again. Yet, at the same time, it's been necessary. I've felt compelled to share because I know I am not the only one who has struggled in this way. If sharing my story can help someone else, then the anguish of putting words to paper, telling it, putting it down in black and white and getting it out there, will be well worth it.

"I cannot do all the good that the world needs.
But the world needs all the good that I can do." ~ Jana Stanfield

Thank you for joining me,
Kay Whiting Harrison

AFTERWORD

———— ◆ ————

I spoke to a friend during the final days of writing this book. She asked permission to ask a personal question. "Of course," I said, "I am an open book. Literally!" She asked if I was still bothered by any suicidal ideation. No, I told her, I do not have any further thoughts of suicide. She contemplated for a moment and then asked, "Why do you think that is?"

Her question surprised me. No one had ever asked me that question directly. It also gave me something to think about. The ideations didn't disappear overnight, nor did the depression, anxiety or mood swings. I have been a work in progress since the day of my attempt. Some days are easier than others. Some days I don't want to think or write about any of this. Some days I binge on movies. Some days I help others who are struggling. Occasionally, I feel triggered and I have to work through some emotional stuff. It hasn't been a walk in the park but I can honestly say this: Surprisingly, opening up and talking about my attempt has been the most freeing thing I've done. Staying silent was definitely the hardest part of my whole journey.

Finding a therapist that I completely trust has been a godsend. Writing this book and speaking to others about my attempt has been unexpectedly therapeutic. Taking classes and learning more about mental health has been helpful. Teaching classes and helping others as a Certified Peer Support Specialist has been deeply fulfilling. I have honest and open communication with my husband and several close friends. I pray. I meditate. I eat a healthy diet (most of the time) and I am compliant with my medications. I never use addictive substances. I spend as much time as I can outdoors. So, when people ask me today how I am doing I can honestly say, "I am doing great" because I am genuinely doing great.

Not every day is peaceful or easy, some days are stressful and challenging, but every day that I make the effort to maintain my mental health is a good day.

ACKNOWLEDGMENTS

————◆————

Wendy O'Leary, my friend, and ghostwriter. Thank you for taking my journals and rough drafts and turning them into a masterpiece. I could not have done this without you.

To my siblings for their support
Carol
Kirk
Anne

To my friends who cheered me on
when worry and doubt clouded my mind
Kendall Mortensen Geiger
Marie Crook Watkins
Susan Webb Kohler

Reviewers

A heartfelt thank you to the reviewers for taking the time and effort to read this manuscript. All of your comments and suggestions helped improve the quality of the book. You are deeply appreciated!

ABOUT THE AUTHOR

———— ◆ ————

Kay Whiting Harrison is a wife, mother, grandmother, sister, businesswoman, avid skier, hiker and bicyclist, and - a suicide attempt survivor. Although it's one of the most difficult things she has done in her life, she shares her personal story to encourage others to open up about their own struggles with mental illness instead of hiding and suffering alone like she did for so many years while trying to care for her family, maintain her career and remain active in her volunteer work with her community and church.

Her struggle with depression and anxiety began at the age of seven. As an adult, the mental illness became debilitating. She feels blessed to have found the right kinds of support, treatment and therapeutic interventions that have literally "saved" her life. She wants others to know that they, too, can recover if they reach out for help.

Kay retired in 2016 from a career in hospital management working with over 300 physicians in three hospitals in California.

Prior to that she was the founder of Common Sense Marketing and Valley Speaker Services. She has twenty-five years experience working in marketing for various companies and was a member of four local chambers of commerce, chairwoman and interim CEO of one. She has been and continues to be an active member of many other community organizations and her church. Kay has been a speaker and presenter for women's and religious organizations for over 25 years.

Today Kay is a Certified Peer Support Specialist in the State of Utah and is certified in Suicide Intervention, QPR, Mental Health First Aid and LEAP. Kay has dedicated her life to assist and support others who suffer. Kay and her husband, Lex speak openly about her mental illness and suicide attempt to groups, churches, individuals, and organizations. She is steadfast in fighting to end the stigma and discrimination that accompanies mental illness.

Kay is from Utah where she attended Weber State University and Brigham Young University. She met Lex, while both were racing for the BYU ski team. They have four children and four grandchildren. They reside in Park City, Utah.

Kay invites you to check out her website where you can connect with her by sending a message and/or find additional resources and information about mental illness and suicide. Groups and organizations can book Kay for a live or virtual speaking engagement.

ABOUT THE CO-WRITER

———— ◆ ————

Wendy O'Leary is a family member whose adult son has both a serious mental illness and a traumatic brain injury that he sustained as a teen when he was hit by a car. She has 17 + years' experience working in mental health advocacy and providing Family Peer Support and Wraparound Certification training and coaching. Wendy has been trained in LEAP, Nurtured Heart Approach, Nonviolent Communication, Motivational Interviewing, Youth Mental Health First Aid and other modalities. She holds a bachelor's degree in Holistic Theology. She is a Certified Family Peer Support Specialist and currently works at NAMI Utah as a Family Mentor and Mental Health Court Advocate.

Wendy has trained many individuals to share their stories in powerful and effective ways. She champions peer and family peer support, believing that the lived experience of individuals and family members is our most valuable asset for creating real change. She is dedicated to "comforting the disturbed and disturbing the comfortable" as she works to address the current 'crisis of care' for and the discrimination against those with serious mental illnesses.

She knows firsthand the burden of care on families which can often prove insurmountable as they become emotionally and physically exhausted and financially wiped out trying to provide the care that is needed for their loved one to engage in treatment and recovery. Without this care, the outcomes for seriously mentally ill individuals are dire - including incarceration, homelessness, poverty, suicide, addictions, and early death from all causes.

Wendy enjoys being a freelance writer. She has published dozens of articles in local and regional magazines and newspapers. She writes about community, social and spiritual issues, including mental health. She has extensive experience developing training curriculums as well as marketing content for both print and digital media.

Wendy lives in beautiful Midway, Utah and enjoys spending as much time outside as she can - hiking, biking, paddle boarding and enjoying nature. Her favorite things to do are road tripping, reading, dancing, and playing pool. Oh, and writing!!!
https://writer4hire.godaddysites.com/
wendymoleary@outlook.com

Part Two

ADVICE AND RESOURCES

PART TWO

ADVICE AND RESOURCES

———————◦◦◦———————

My hope is that you gleaned something - perhaps just a tidbit of wisdom, a glimmer of hope or some personally significant insight from reading my story. I also hope that you are now feeling a sense of connection with me and with my intention to support those who are struggling with mental illness and their loved ones.

When I support someone who is struggling, I listen to understand who they are and what they are going through and what kind of support or help they are looking for before I offer any suggestions or advice. In fact, I try not to give any unsolicited advice. Oftentimes, people who are struggling just want someone who can really see and hear them, really understand how they are feeling and someone who can accept them without giving advice. They want to be acknowledged and validated.

Therefore, this second section is completely optional. You may choose to put the book down and be finished with it for good. You may choose to put it down and come back later. You might feel compelled to contact me through my website. Or you might wish to browse the topics in this section and only read the ones that you feel are relevant to you or the ones that you would like some advice and resources on. It's up to you. My sincerest wish is for you to be encouraged from reading my story to take a step toward healing by reaching out to someone if you are suffering. And if you are trying to help someone else who is suffering, my sincerest wish is that you review the Advice and Resources in this section and choose what feels helpful in your efforts to support another.

1. Resources and Advice for Family Members
2. Resources and Advice for Persons with Mental Health Challenges
3. Advice for Those Struggling with Suicidal Thoughts
4. What to Say to Someone Who May be Suicidal
5. What to Say When Someone has Lost a Loved One to Suicide
6. The Language We Use About Suicide Matters
7. PTSD and Complex Trauma
8. Toxic Relationships and Mental Illness
9. Bullying and Mental Illness
10. Perfectionism and Mental Illness
11. Myths and Spiritual Beliefs about Suicide
12. Dangers of High Functioning Depression

13. How to Find a "Good" Therapist
14. What to do in a Mental Health Crisis
15. Peer Support

PLEASE NOTE:

All the links found in this book will be posted on my website for easy access

www.thrivingaftersuicideattempt.com

Chapter One:

ADVICE AND RESOURCES FOR FAMILY MEMBERS

———— ◆ ————

Reflections from Lex:
"What I Learned as a Family Member"

I thought I was doing the right thing all those years, dealing with Kay's depression and anxiety on my own, without seeking support for myself. I think it was because I didn't want anyone to know what she was going through. She cared so much about others and not wanting to be a burden to anyone that she would always put on a happy face in public. They couldn't see her struggle, but I could. As things worsened, I worried more but I didn't know what to do differently to help her. So, I kept trying to do what I had always done.

We would talk things over. I did some research and read some books on depression and mood disorders. I thought

I was protecting Kay by not letting others know about her struggles. I also kept rationalizing that it wasn't that bad. After all, she was well-liked in the community, working full-time, serving in our church and with non-profit agencies. She had many good weeks in between bouts of serious depression and anxiety.

I didn't talk to any of my friends, relatives or church leaders because I didn't think it was my place to reveal what Kay was going through. I especially didn't want to tarnish her reputation with anyone. I didn't want anyone to think less of Kay because of her inner struggles. I now realize this is what stigma does. It causes us to be ashamed to speak out.

I've always admired Kay's headstrong determination and persistence. She has high standards for herself and wants to do things well. These are positive personality traits. At the same time, these traits also caused her to put too much pressure on herself at times. She tends to be a perfectionist. I've since learned that when a perfectionist feels anxious, they think the solution is to do more - whether it is more organizing, cleaning, working or whatever it is that makes them feel better about themselves. This can become a vicious cycle.

Also, at first, I didn't recognize what Kay was dealing with was a serious mental illness. It took a very long time for this realization to slowly settle in, along with the knowledge that this is something we must take seriously and we will need to manage for the rest of our lives.

When I finally opened up and talked to others and received support, it was a huge relief. Looking back, I know that I did it wrong. I was trying to protect her yet I should have reached out for help and support much sooner. I thought I would be betraying Kay if I told someone what I was going through myself. That was a mistake. That was caused by the stigma of mental illness.

I also thought incorrectly that I could get her through this - that I could "fix" this. I'm a fixer. I fix problems all day at work and I thought I could fix this, too. I was wrong. I have finally learned and accepted the fact that I can't fix it. I can hold space. I can listen. No one asks to be mentally ill. Our loved ones with mental illness need our support and understanding. I now tell family members and caregivers that they too need support and it's okay to reach out for help, nor just for your loved one, but for yourself, too. I remind them that they can't fix it and they can't go it alone.

I started speaking to audiences with Kay about mental illness, suicide and the lessons I learned along the way. The reason I speak out is because people don't know what they don't know. I don't want them to make the same mistakes I made. I don't want others to carry with them the "if onlys" the way I do. If only, I had known better than to believe she was getting better that morning before I left, if only, I had known that it wasn't safe to leave her alone that day, if only, I had been more attuned to her real mental and emotional states, if only, I had reached out for support and help for myself or for her sooner, if only, I had taken her to the hospital the night before...

I have since learned how to be more helpful by listening to understand Kay, instead of trying to fix her. I have continued learning and reading books. After reading about L.E.A.P. (Listen, Empathize, Agree, Partner) by Dr. Xavier Amador, I can see how early on I triggered her a lot because I didn't understand how to relate to her when she was depressed or anxious.

As with other kinds of chronic illnesses, the same is true with Kay's illness. She will always have it and it will have to be managed the rest of her life. There is always an awareness of it and the need to manage it. The highs and lows still come and go but they are more manageable now and fewer and farther between. She also has some physical chronic pain issues and the same principle of lifelong management applies.

In my opinion these are the things that have made the biggest difference for Kay:

1. Reducing the pressure (leaving a very stressful job)
2. Compliance with medications
3. Therapy
4. Being physically active
5. Speaking out and talking openly with others

Speaking out has been very therapeutic. I was surprised that speaking up about Kay's mental illness and suicide attempt would be such a relief! But opening up meant not having to hide or be ashamed of anything. We have both received a lot of support as a result.

It was a miracle that Kay survived the attempt. As a result, our faith has grown stronger and so have we. Speaking out has given meaning and purpose to something we used to try to keep hidden due to stigma.

Stigma can prevent you from getting help for someone you love. You think you can handle it. You think you can help them. But you can't keep doing it alone. Stigma can prevent you from seeking the support you need to help your loved one. It's so important to face your fear of speaking up and getting the necessary help.

Kay and I have come a long way since that day she attempted to end her life. We have a better understanding of mental illness and how to manage it. I think I am better able to support Kay now and she is better at managing her own moods and symptoms. Together we talk to audiences about what we've learned. Kay speaks with individuals who are struggling with depression, anxiety and suicidal ideation. I speak with family members who are trying to help them.

RESOURCES

There are many helpful local and regional organizations that provide targeted support and resources for family members who are struggling to help someone with mental illness. Be sure to look online for what is available in your area. Also, check with your local or state health and human service agencies to see if there are **Certified Family Peer Support Specialists** available to assist your family.

Here are four of the most helpful national resources we have found. Most have local chapters, classes and/or resources available to help family members and other community members who are helping someone with mental health challenges.

LEAP® (Listen-Empathize-Agree-Partner) is a science-based communication program to help you create relationships with people who are unable to understand they are ill, with the goal of helping them accept treatment. For more information and free videos: https://www.leapinstitute.org/ https://hacenter.org/home

NAMI (National Alliance on Mental Illness) Family members and caregivers often play a large role in helping and supporting the millions of people in the U.S. who experience mental health conditions each year. The challenges of mental illness do not only affect an individual's family members but also friends, teachers, neighbors, coworkers and others in the community. NAMI provides information and support to anyone who provides emotional, financial or practical support to a person with a mental health condition. Whether you're providing a lot of assistance or very little, the information here can help you better understand the issues that you might face. You can also find local chapters with classes and support groups for families. https://nami.org/Your-Journey/Family-Members-and-Caregivers

Treatment Advocacy Center has been participating in the improvement of treatment laws in the U.S. for twenty-two years. It serves as a watchdog and champion for expanded treatment options, raises public awareness around treatment issues and provides advocacy information to family members who are seeking to help a loved one with serious mental illness who is unwilling or unable to recognize a need for treatment. Click on the 'GET HELP' button and receive comprehensive information on how to help someone in crisis, how to stay safe and how to prepare for mental health emergencies. https://www.treatmentadvocacycenter.org/

National Action Alliance for Prevention of Suicide is working with more than 250 national partners from the public and private sectors to advance the National Strategy for Suicide Prevention (National Strategy). The Action Alliance is currently focusing on three priority areas, selected from the National Strategy, based on their potential to save lives: transforming health systems, transforming communities, and changing the conversation. https://theactionalliance.org/

How to Support Someone with Depression: Recognizing it, What to Say, How to Help https://findyourwords.org/support-someone-with-depression/

All the links found in this book will be posted on my website for easy access
www.thrivingaftersuicideattempt.com

Chapter Two:

ADVICE AND RESOURCES FOR PERSONS WITH MENTAL HEALTH CHALLENGES

———————◆———————

Reflections from Kay:
"What I Learned as a Person with Mental Illness"

I've already shared much of the wisdom I've gleaned from my experiences with anxiety, depression, PTSD and my attempted suicide. If I could impart one more word of advice, it would be this:

There is no shame in asking for help when you are feeling overwhelmed or depressed and don't know what to do. There is also no shame when there is a need for medication. Unfortunately, I know too many individuals who do not understand that mental illness is a real illness and as a result do not seek treatment of any kind.

One mother of a 19 year old told me her daughter was diagnosed with bipolar and refused to get out of bed. I asked if her daughter was getting any kind of treatment or therapy. She said 'no'. I asked if she was on any kind of medication. The mother explained that she, the mother, did not believe in medication for such things. She let me know that there was no point in further discussing medication. This left me wondering if this mother believed that mental illness actually exists. I felt nothing short of complete sadness for this young woman.

RESOURCES

There are many helpful local and regional organizations that provide targeted support and resources for individuals who are struggling with mental health challenges. Be sure to look online to see what is available in your area. Also, check with your local and state health and human service agencies to find out if there are **Certified Peer Support Specialists** available in your area to work with you. Here are some helpful national resources. Many have local chapters you can connect with.

National Alliance on Mental Illness. Learn what to do if you've been diagnosed with a mental illness and what it means. You can get support, education and information on a variety of topics including, how and when to disclose, what to do in a crisis, taking care of yourself, navigating finances and work and more. You can also find local chapters where you can take classes, share your story, and meet others who have similar experiences and mental health challenges. https://nami.org/Your-Journey/Individuals-with-Mental-Illness

Recovery International. The mission of Recovery International is to use the cognitive-behavioral, peer-to-peer, self-help training system developed by Abraham Low, MD, to help individuals gain skills to lead more peaceful and productive lives. Recovery International hosts meetings that provide a safe space to receive guidance, fellowship, acceptance, and support from peers with similar problems. All meetings follow the Recovery 4-Step Method that addresses the underlying cause of most symptoms. Through the structured meeting and encouragement from their peers, participants learn to "spot" their angry and fearful temper and use their will-power to manage symptoms and lead productive, healthier lives. This method has helped people learn to identify and manage negative thoughts, feelings, beliefs, and behaviors that can lead to emotional distress and related physical symptoms. Most meetings are online. To learn more: https://recoveryinternational.org/newcomer/

What is Cognitive Behavioral Therapy?
https://www.apa.org/ptsd-guideline/patients-and-families/cognitive-behavioral

Five more mental health resources that can #BeTheDifference when you need it most:

- The National Suicide Prevention Line. **This hotline provides free, confidential support 24/7 to people in distress across the United States. Call 988 or 1-800-273-TALK (8255) for support.**

- The SAMHSA Helpline. **SAMHSA's National Helpline is a free, confidential information service that provides treatment and support referrals 24/7 to people facing mental illness and addictions. Call 1-800-662-HELP (4357) for support.**

- Crisis Text Line. **Crisis Text Line provides free, confidential support via text message 24/7 to those in crisis situations. Text HOME to 741741 for support.**

- The Trevor Project. **The Trevor Project provides free, confidential support 24/7 to LGBTQ youth via a helpline, text and online instant messaging system. Call 1-866-488-7386 for support.**

- The Veterans Crisis Line. **The Veterans Crisis line provides free, confidential support 24/7 to veterans, all service members and their family and friends in times of need. Call 1-800-273-8255 and press 1 or text 838255 for support**

All the links found in this book will be posted on my website for easy access

www.thrivingaftersuicideattempt.com

Chapter Three.

HELP FOR THOSE STRUGGLING WITH SUICIDAL THOUGHTS

———— ◆ ————

ADVICE

I've talked to some individuals who have expressed to me they have intrusive or obsessive thoughts of taking their own lives. This is very distressing, to be sure. If you have this experience, of continual or frequent thoughts of suicide, please, please, please let someone know. Someone you trust. Someone who loves you. Or if you prefer, you can call and speak with someone on a suicide prevention or crisis hotline and let them know what you are going through. Please know that this is a symptom of depression and/or another mental illness and it can be treated.

RESOURCES

If you're in crisis, there are options available to help you cope. You can also call the Lifeline at any time to speak to someone and get support, whether you are in crisis or just need to talk with someone. For confidential support available 24/7 for everyone in the United States, call 988 or 1-800-273-8255. You can also text "WORDS" to 741741 if you would rather text, than talk.

Some steps you can take to HELP YOURSELF include finding a therapist or support group, building and using a personal network of support, making a safety plan and learning more about each of these steps.

For more information, please visit:

How to Help Yourself. Suicide Prevention Lifeline
https://suicidepreventionlifeline.org/help-yourself/

How to Get Help with Depression and Suicidal Thoughts
https://findyourwords.org/depression-help/suicidal-thoughts/
Resilience and Mental Health
https://findyourwords.org/self-care/

Understanding Depression: Signs and How to get Help
https://findyourwords.org/understanding-depression/

All the links found in this book will be posted on my website for easy access
www.thrivingaftersuicideattempt.com

Chapter Four.

WHAT TO SAY TO SOMEONE WHO MAY BE SUICIDAL

————— ◆ —————

ADVICE

I was called to help with a woman who suffered from alcoholism, and was refusing to go to her scheduled treatment center. When I arrived she was conscious but intoxicated. I called her by name and softly talked to her. I asked her the following questions: Will you come with us to the treatment center? "No". Do you hurt anywhere? "No". Are you thinking of hurting yourself? "Yes". Do you have a plan? "Yes". Do you want to die? "Yes".

At this point I called 911 and asked for the Mobile Crisis Outreach Team (MCOT) to come. MCOT is a team of mental health professionals, along with a peer support specialist who respond to people in mental health crisis. Law enforcement and paramedics may be dispatched as needed.

It's important NOT to avoid the subject of suicide if you think someone is extremely depressed or has expressed suicidal thoughts. Here are three resources that can help guide a conversation with someone who may be suicidal.

RESOURCES

Question, Persuade, Refer. https://qprinstitute.com/
Be the One to ASK!
https://www.bethe1to.com/bethe1to-steps-evidence/
National Suicide Prevention.
https://suicidepreventionlifeline.org/

All the links found in this book will be posted on my website for easy access
www.thrivingaftersuicideattempt.com

Chapter Five.

WHAT TO SAY WHEN SOMEONE HAS LOST A LOVED ONE TO SUICIDE

ADVICE

I personally know too many families who have lost a loved one to suicide over the past five years. People are often at loss as to what to say or do. As a result, many times they don't say or do anything, which can be devastating and cause the grieving family member to feel isolated, alienated and sometimes even judged.

Granted, there are no words that can adequately console someone whose loved one took their own life. The mixture of intense emotions are swirling back and forth between guilt, remorse, grief, anger and sometimes shock and disbelief. May I offer a suggestion of what to say, which is simply, "I'm so sorry - so very sorry for what you are going through!" Period. Said with heartfelt warmth this simple sentence can acknowledge to the person that you care and provides some comfort in a very difficult time.

RESOURCES

Here is an excerpt from an article (see link below) about how to talk to someone who has lost a loved one to suicide:

Seven things you can say:

- I am so sorry for your loss.
- I know how much you love _____. This must be so hard.
- I want you to feel safe sharing anything with me. Do you want to talk about it?
- It's okay if you don't want to talk right now. I am here to listen whenever you are ready.
- Can I make dinner/do laundry/run that errand (specific task) for you?
- I remember that time when…. (Don't be afraid to talk about the person)
- You can grieve as long and as hard as you need to and I will be here for you.

Things you want to avoid saying:

- Oh no! What happened?
- I know exactly how you feel!
- They're in a better place now.

Remember, that it's more important to be a fully present listener than to figure out exactly what to say. For more information read the full article here: https://www.self.com/story/help-friend-suicide-loss-survivor

American Foundation for Suicide Prevention has helpful information on how to support someone who has lost someone to suicide. https://afsp.org/story/10-ways-to-support-a-loved-one-who-has-lost-someone-to-suicide

All the links found in this book will be posted on my website for easy access

www.thrivingaftersuicideattempt.com

Chapter Six.

THE LANGUAGE WE USE ABOUT SUICIDE MATTERS:

The Power of Words

————— ◆ —————

ADVICE

Why We Don't Say 'Committed Suicide.' Dr. Xavier Amador explains, "The research on the brain dysfunction is abundantly clear; people suffering from mental illness do not commit suicide or kill themselves. Those phrases suggest a knowingly and voluntary choice. Nothing could be further from the truth. Instead, they die from a suicide just like people die from cancer or heart disease."

"For example, the phrase "committed suicide" is frowned on because it harks back to an era when suicide was considered a sin or a crime. Think about the times when we use the word "commit": "commit adultery" or "commit murder." Similarly, "successful suicide" or "unsuccessful attempt" are considered poor word choices because they connote an achievement of something positive, even though they result in tragic outcomes."

"Suicide prevention is a hard sell. As a result, well-meaning health professionals often make serious errors when crafting messages for suicide prevention. We have a tendency to think that we need to grab the public's attention through graphic and scary messages when that just tends to turn people off. Instead, we need to think about aligning with our audience's beliefs, values, priorities, and needs. We must craft messages that are positively engaging, providing people with the information we want them to remember, and give them action steps."

"Instead of just "raising awareness" by sharing statistics of suicide death, we can inspire hope by sharing stories of recovery and letting them know that help is available. Kevin Hines's story is one that spreads a ripple of hope around the world. Mr. Hines survived a jump off the Golden Gate Bridge, and his BuzzFeed video now has over 8 million views on YouTube. His main message—you are not alone, and brain health is possible. He is a fierce advocate for mental wellness and lives his message of fighting for a passion for life every day." (See link to Kevin's story below).

"We must talk about suicide if we are going to get in front of it. But HOW we talk about suicide matters. Unsafe messages and data that leave us feeling that "suicide is an epidemic" can create harm. Instead, let's focus on messages and stories that inspire hope and healing, and share resources that help people through their despair."

RESOURCES

To better understand individuals who have died or tried to die by suicide, please read the full article (link below) which covers the following topics:

- Putting People First
- The Myth That Suicide Is Selfish
- The Myth That It Was Their Choice
- Getting Positive Messages out There: Hope, Strength, and Healing
- Crafting Effective Messages About Suicide: Hope is the Antidote

https://www.irmi.com/articles/expert-commentary/language-matters-committed-suicide

Words Matter. A Guide: Learning to Talk About Suicide in a Hopeful and Respectful Way that Has the Power to Save Lives (from the Center for Addiction and Mental Health). This is a comprehensive four-page printable/downloadable guide.

https://www.camh.ca/-/media/files/words-matter-suicide-language-guide.pdf

The 2%: THE KEVIN HINES STORY

https://www.relias.com/resource/2-percent-kevin-hines-story

All the links found in this book will be posted on my website for easy access
www.thrivingaftersuicideattempt.com

Chapter Seven.

POST-TRAUMATIC STRESS DISORDER AND COMPLEX TRAUMA

———————— ◆ ————————

ADVICE

When we have an experience that overwhelms our capacity to process it and let it go, it remains within our nervous system and cellular memory, waiting to be triggered, re-experienced and hopefully, this time, processed and released. However, if we are not aware that we are being triggered and having trauma responses to ordinary situations in life, we may find ourselves over-reacting and/or feeling unusual amounts of fear, doubt and worry and not know why. This can have a cumulative effect and oftentimes leads to serious depression and anxiety.

This is what trauma - unprocessed negative experiences - does to us. This disorder is called post-traumatic stress disorder and, in cases where long-term toxic relationships and/or bullying have caused repeated negative experiences, it is called "complex trauma."

A large part of my healing came from understanding how early trauma affects our neurology. I had always thought that PTSD was something that war veterans or persons who had lived through extreme and horrible childhood abuse and neglect dealt with. My therapist, Bobbi Fosburg, helped me understand that anyone can suffer from PTSD since trauma is, in fact, a human response to an experience, of any kind, that overwhelms your current capacity to process it. It stays with you and has a cumulative effect on your nervous system and your mental and emotional well-being.

I was surprised and relieved when Bobbi explained how my early experiences could, in effect, rewire my brain in such a way that led me to become more susceptible to the pressures of life and subsequently, to developing serious depression, anxiety and mood disorders, than someone with a neuro-typical brain. And it didn't take being a victim of severe child abuse or being a war veteran to be affected by PTSD. She referred to post-war and other severe trauma as the Big "T" and all other trauma as the Little "t". She did not minimize the little "t" and explained that it can be just as traumatizing and damaging as the Big "T".

RESOURCES
Eye Movement Desensitization and Reprocessing (EMDR) worked wonderfully for me and within several months

my trauma had completely subsided. For more information about PTSD, EMDR and Complex Trauma, please visit these websites:

PTSD Examined. The Five Types of Post Traumatic Stress Disorder
https://bestdaypsych.com/ptsd-examined-the-five-types-of-post-traumatic-stress-disorder/
What is EMDR? From the EMDR Institute, Inc.
https://www.emdr.com/what-is-emdr/
What is Complex PTSD? Symptoms, Treatment and Resources
https://www.medicalnewstoday.com/articles/322886#symptoms

All the links found in this book will be posted on my website for easy access
www.thrivingaftersuicideattempt.com

Chapter Eight:

TOXIC RELATIONSHIPS AND MENTAL ILLNESS

---◆---

ADVICE

Many people who suffer from trauma often have trouble discerning who they can trust and who they can't trust. This, along with other complex psychological factors, sometimes contributes to trying to make relationships work with people who do not have your best interests at heart, resulting in further trauma.

I have been in several toxic relationships. I wish I had learned years ago how to provide myself with the supportive self-talk needed to deal with these relationships and the ability to follow through on it. I needed to mentally say, "You don't deserve my energy or my time. I'm taking it back." I have had to walk away or remove myself, as much as possible, from these relationships in order to succeed. It is hard, yes, but so worth the sense of an intact self and peace of mind!

According to clinical psychologist Gillian Needleman, "A toxic relationship is basically an unhealthy relationship or friendship." The relationship could be with a friend, family member, or even a partner or ex-partner. "You're unable to have a meaningful and positive connection with the other person and this often leaves you questioning yourself."

How you feel before or after spending time with a person is a great way to measure if your relationship with them is healthy or not.

"In a toxic friendship scenario, you might always feel emotionally drained after seeing them; it can be a real energy drain, a feeling of heaviness," says Ms Needleman. "You might feel a huge sense of obligation or guilt for not seeing them enough. You might be dreading the interaction, knowing that a conversation is all about them, or a stream of criticism lies ahead."

Ms Needleman says that the impacts of a toxic relationship should not be underestimated. They can affect your sense of self and identity, damage your self-esteem, and even lead to feelings of depression and/or anxiety.

"You can be left feeling inadequate, or somehow flawed," she says. "If an important person in your life is always putting you down, you're getting direct criticism. In a toxic relationship, it can feel like who you are, or what you do, is never enough."

To read more about how to remedy a toxic relationship and protect your mental health, please check out the following articles:

RESOURCES

Are You in a Toxic Relationship?
https://www.nowtolove.com.au/relationships/relationship-advice/are-you-in-a-toxic-relationship-56944
Gillian Needleman: How Toxic Friends Affect Your Mental Health
https://bedlamite.co/2021/01/27/how-toxic-friends-affect-your-mental-health/
10 Signs of an Unhealthy (Toxic) Relationship
https://www.ramseysolutions.com/relationships/toxic-relationship-signs

All the links found in this book will be posted on my website for easy access
www.thrivingaftersuicideattempt.com

Chapter Nine.

BULLYING AND MENTAL ILLNESS

———— ◆ ————

ADVICE

Bullying fits into the category of "Toxic Relationships" because it is an unhealthy relationship that takes a toll on your mental and emotional wellbeing. However, bullying is in a special category of its own because it involves sustained and intentional overt or covert manipulations designed to beat you down for the purpose of the bully getting something they want.

There are classroom bullies and workplace bullies and they can detrimentally affect an entire group of people causing great harm to the individuals they target as well as closing off any possibility of the satisfaction that comes from successful learning and/or genuine collaboration and teamwork.

Workplace, schoolyard and cyber-bullying is not uncommon and can cause grave psychological harm to the recipient and the onlookers.

My own experiences with being bullied came from a neighborhood bully when I was a child. This bullying occurred periodically and I had no idea how it was impacting my self-esteem until I attended therapy and made the connection between that experience and the experience of being bullied in my job years later.

My boss often demeaned me in front of others and I felt powerless to speak up, just as I couldn't speak up as a child being bullied. I couldn't think clearly while it was happening and I didn't think anyone would listen or care about what I had to say because of the power differential that existed. After all, the boss was from a national corporate office and much higher up on the totem pole than me.

The anxiety became unrelenting because no matter how hard I tried, I felt powerless to stand up to him. The resulting stress affected the quality of my work, causing more anxiety and pressure. I found out that when an underlying mental illness meets active bullying, the results can be profound, even deadly.

For more information and resources on how to cope with bullying, please check out the following resources.

RESOURCES
The Effects of Bullying/Stop Bullying.gov
Bullying.govhttps://www.stopbullying.gov/bullying/effects

Bullying vs Discrimination: How To Tell The Difference in the Workplace https://www.empowerwork.org/blog/bullying-vs-discrimination-how-to-tell-the-difference-in-the-workplace
How To Deal With Adult Bullying https://www.verywellmind.com/how-to-deal-with-adult-bullying-5187158

All the links found in this book will be posted on my website for easy access

www.thrivingaftersuicideattempt.com

Chapter Ten.

PERFECTIONISM AND MENTAL ILLNESS

———— ◆ ————

ADVICE

While I was preparing to speak to a church women's group, the person who invited me to speak asked if I could also talk about the danger of perfectionism. I thought about this and talked to Lex. I did some research, and then called my friend, Xavier Amador for his input. As I opened myself and listened to what they were telling me, bells started to ring and red flags started to wave. It dawned on me for the first time that my tendency toward perfectionism during my career had helped push me over the edge.

What a surprise! I had never considered myself to be a perfectionist. Not once did I consider myself ever doing anything perfectly well. What a huge eye-opener it was for me to recognize my own tendency toward perfectionism. Not only did I talk about it during my presentation but I shared how toxic this tendency had been for me most of my life.

I began to understand more and more about the relationship of perfectionist thinking and the impact it has on your mental health. I was very grateful to Dr. Xavier Amador for his insights. I would like to share with you what he sent to me about this topic:

"What happens when you're a perfectionist is that you develop a very narrow beam of attention and a tunnel vision when you're feeling like you haven't done a good enough job. When you're feeling anxious you think the solution is to clean more or to organize more or to do more for your children."

"You may not realize this but you're paying a price for that tunnel vision for that pursuit of perfectionism. The price you pay is not being aware of emotions. Add to that the fact that one out of five Americans suffer from serious mental illnesses and you could be blindsided by illnesses like depression anxiety disorders because of this. And the biggest problem with perfectionism is that none of us are perfect; we are always going to fail at being perfect. And that adds an added burden of guilt and sadness and anxiety. So abandon perfectionism and open your mind and heart to the full range of emotions that you're feeling and you will be better equipped to deal with any mental illness should it come your way." ~ **Dr. Xavier Amador; Professor of Psychiatry and Clinical Psychology at Columbia University and Director of Psychology at the New York State Psychiatric Institute. President and Founder of the Henry Amador / LEAP Foundation**

RESOURCES

Perfectionism: Symptoms, Treatment and Prevention
https://www.healthline.com/health/perfectionism

The Negative Effects of Perfectionism: How Getting Things 'Just Right' Can Be So Wrong
https://www.vetxinternational.com/the-negative-effects-of-perfectionism-how-getting-things-just-right-can-be-so-wrong/

All the links found in this book will be posted on my website for easy access
www.thrivingaftersuicideattempt.com

Chapter Eleven.

MYTHS AND SPIRITUAL BELIEFS ABOUT SUICIDE

---◆---

ADVICE

Mental illness is just that... It is an illness of the brain. I would like to share with you what I learned after researching my own religious beliefs. I hope that you will find comfort in this, as I have.

The author Jane Clayson Johnson in 'Silent Souls Weeping', says that many people, "often feel left adrift, uncertain what suicide means for a loved one's salvation and their own family's eternal status. The stinging stigma attached to mental illness and suicide aggravates the already intense pain of grief. Questions plague the mind."

In 2018, my church leaders released a series of videos addressing this very topic and vocalizing a pressing need to do all we can to prevent suicide, to minister to those who have suicidal thoughts or who have attempted suicide, and to support those who are left behind when a loved one does take his or her life.

One of my church leaders, Dale G. Renland, says, "There's an old sectarian notion that suicide is a sin and that someone who commits suicide is banished to hell forever. *That is totally false!* I believe that the vast majority of cases will find that these individuals have lived heroic lives and that suicide will not be a defining characteristic of their eternities."

Jane Clayson Johnson continues, "It is not our place to judge. It is our place to love. It is our place to mourn with those who suffer from the dark feelings of suicidal ideation and those who are left behind when those feelings result in action. This is one of the most difficult losses a family can experience. It should harrow up our deepest feelings of compassion and stir us up from the sidelines to active, truly charitable, and supportive sharing of its crushing burden. There is no place for condemnation. Gossip or shunning. There is room for prevention, and for communication."

Suicide should not be swept under a rug. Just as it is never good to box up and ignore our feelings, it is never good to keep silent about suicidal thoughts and mental health in general. The notion that talking to someone about their feelings may lead people to act on them had been debunked by numerous studies, as well as by those who have attempted suicide and survived. Talking about suicide can actually help prevent it. Not talking about it, neglecting to talk about it, sends the message that they can't talk about it. It's important to talk about feelings of depression, or fantasies about suicide, which can certainly fester inside, if they're not talking about more openly.

This is what I, Kay, wish someone had said to me before my attempt, "Are you thinking of harming yourself? Are you thinking of suicide?" I would have said yes and that would have opened up a lifesaving dialogue. I believed no one asked because no one knew about my depression and anxiety. Although Lex knew I was struggling, he did not comprehend the seriousness of my mental state. I carefully kept it hidden from everyone.

<u>Never be afraid to ask.</u> If you suspect a loved one may be more depressed than they are letting on and/or may be considering suicide, please ask them. Start a dialogue with them.

RESOURCES

NAMI - National Alliance on Mental Illness - Faith and Spirituality

As we learn more and more about the connections between the mind and body, it becomes clear that spirituality, religion and faith can help some individuals live well with mental health conditions. Some individuals and families turn to faith in times of crisis to help in their recovery while others find that spiritual practices help them continue to manage their mental health.

How Faith Can Help

Some people find that religion and individual spirituality have a positive impact on their physical and mental health.

What Makes A Good Faith Community A Welcoming Community?

Each world religion has its own set of ideas and practices. If you grew up in a specific faith and feel comfortable with it, you may already have prayers and rituals that support your health. If you feel alienated from your faith of origin, you may feel uncertain whether you can benefit from faith. Just as there isn't a downside to learning more about your mental health condition, there's no downside to learning more about religion or spirituality. Learning about a faith doesn't obligate you to follow it and may give you new ideas for how to live with a mental health condition.

If you're looking for a regular place to worship or practice your faith, be alert to how each congregation or community approaches mental health conditions. Some churches view mental illness as a moral failing for which prayer is the only treatment while others maintain active outreach programs for people with mental health conditions. Above all, find a community where you feel welcomed and loved despite your mental health condition. Finding a caring congregation that is accepting and supports your healing journey is key.

https://www.NAMI.org/Your-Journey/Individuals-with-Mental-Illness/Faith-Spirituality

Jewish Nations Action Alliance - Faith, Hope, Life; Celebrating Reasons to Live

Judaism teaches that how people are born and how they die are in God's hands. Life belongs to God, not to the individual. It is a gift to be treasured. Taking one's own life is viewed as a serious violation of one's responsibility to God and society. Although Jewish teachings do not condone suicide, Jews tend not to blame people who die by suicide. Instead, they seek to understand. The suicide is condemned, but not the person. In general, Jews believe that most suicides can be prevented if actions are taken in time—such as giving a person food and water, personal affirmations, and physical comfort, and getting the person the care he or she needs.
https://theactionalliance.org/faith-hope-life/religion-specific-materials/jewish

Christian Religion Action Alliance - Faith, Hope, Life; Celebrating Reasons to Live

Christian religions today acknowledge that suicide is often the result of untreated depression, pain, or other suffering. People of Christian faith seek not to blame the person who dies by suicide, but to provide care to those at risk, survivors, and their families. A Christian perspective on suicide begins with an affirmation of faith that nothing, including suicide, separates us from the love of God.

https://theactionalliance.org/communities/faith-communities

Talk to Your Faith Community/Religious Leader.

If you are a member of a faith community, speak to the administrative staff and/or leaders of the church and see if there are counseling sessions and/or mental health resources that your church can make available to help you support your loved one with a mental illness.

All the links found in this book will be posted on my website for easy access

www.thrivingaftersuicideattempt.com

Chapter Twelve:

THE DANGERS OF HAVING A HIGH FUNCTIONING MENTAL ILLNESS

———— ◆ ————

ADVICE

Over the course of my life, I made sure that only my family and therapist/doctor knew what I was experiencing. I rarely talked about it to anyone else. Much of the time, I really was happy and fun, and when I was struggling and spiraling, I kept it within the boundaries of my home.

After my suicide attempt when I began talking and speaking openly about my illness, my friends were astonished because they rarely saw me as anything but happy and outgoing. They couldn't believe the inner battle that I had been fighting. There were times when that battle was raging inside but I always had a smile on my face. This proved to be very dangerous for me.

I wasn't intentionally hiding my inner struggles but I kept thinking I could handle them privately. Because I was high functioning, I was able to continue working and being an active member of my church and community, until one day, I couldn't. I hope that my story will help those who are likewise struggling internally and putting on a happy face externally to realize they need to address their inner turmoil sooner, rather than later. It's okay to ask for help. It's braver than acting like everything is okay, when it's not.

RESOURCES

The following articles can help you identify if you are struggling with a high functioning mental illness and provide additional resources and advice for you to look into.

This is What High Functioning Depression Looks Like
https://www.healthline.com/health/depression/this-is-what-high-functioning-depression-looks-like

High Functioning Mental Health Disorders
https://www.mentalhealthcenter.org/high-functioning-mental-health-disorders/

All the links found in this book will be posted on my website for easy access
www.thrivingaftersuicideattempt.com

Chapter Thirteen:

HOW TO FIND A "GOOD" THERAPIST

———— ♦ ————

ADVICE

It's important to realize that not all therapists are equally helpful. Therapists often have areas of specialty - specific skills, expertise and experience with different types of mental illnesses and/or different populations (i.e. women/men, youth/adults, LGBTQ/straight, etc.) A large part of the therapeutic process is contained in the relationship between you and your therapist and that's why it is vital to select a therapist that you genuinely connect with, like and trust.

Granted, you might be limited in your selection of available therapists due to insurance and/or funding but do what you can to ensure that your therapist is someone you can relate to and has expertise with the types of issues you need help with.

RESOURCES

One of the best resources for finding a therapist who is a good fit for you can be found at Psychology Today website where you can search for Therapists, Psychiatrists, Treatment Centers, Teletherapy, and Support Groups in your area. You can learn about each therapist or treatment center, their philosophy and approaches, specialty areas, what insurances they take and more! If you aren't interested in therapy, check out the variety of support groups in your area using this link. **https://www.psychologytoday.com/us/therapists**

Nine Tips for Finding the Right Therapist
https://www.healthline.com/health/how-to-find-a-therapist

All the links found in this book will be posted on my website for easy access

www.thrivingaftersuicideattempt.com

Chapter Fourteen:

WHAT TO DO IN A MENTAL HEALTH CRISIS

———— ◆ ————

ADVICE

It's often difficult to know the best way to help someone who is experiencing a mental health crisis and/or when to intervene and seek professional assistance. It's best to familiarize yourself with the crisis resources available in your area BEFORE there is a mental health crisis.

If you are with someone in crisis and you are not sure what to do, don't be afraid to call a crisis hotline and let the crisis worker know about the situation and your concerns. They can help you assess whether a professional intervention is called for.

If someone in a mental health crisis is threatening their own or another's safety and/or has ingested something or harmed themselves in a potentially life threatening way, call 911 immediately. Let dispatch know that the person is experiencing a mental health crisis.

RESOURCES

Local Crisis Hotline - Call or visit the website of the Health Department for your County and out what the local mental health crisis hotline number is for your area.

MCOT (Mobile Crisis Outreach Teams) - Check and see if your area has Mobile Crisis Outreach Teams available to someone in a mental health crisis. These are multi-disciplinary teams that usually consist of a therapist, a peer support and the police are often available on standby in case they are needed. The team is specifically trained in crisis response and the goal of the team is to quietly and non-intrusively bring support to the person in crisis, preventing further trauma. They go to where the person is and visit with them, do an assessment, provide appropriate intervention, including safety planning and follow up care. They can also make referrals to a higher level of care if needed.

CIT - (Crisis Intervention Trained) - Many law enforcement officers have been trained in mental health crisis intervention. See if your local law enforcement agencies have trained officers. If so, when calling 911 due to a mental health emergency, be sure to ask specifically for a CIT Officer to be dispatched and emphasize that it is a mental health emergency. On July 22, 2022 the new National Mental Health Emergency number 988 was activated.

All the links found in this book will be posted on my website for easy access
www.thrivingaftersuicideattempt.com

Chapter Fifteen:

PEER SUPPORT

ADVICE

A peer support specialist is a person with "lived experience" who has been trained to support those who struggle with mental health challenges, psychological trauma and/or substance use. Their personal experience with these challenges provides them with a kind of expertise that professionals cannot replicate, no matter how skilled or empathetic they may be.

Family peers are parents, spouses and siblings of loved ones with a mental illness. They have the "lived experience" of supporting someone they love who is struggling, including finding resources and treatment. They understand the challenges involved in caring for someone who has mental health challenges.

Peer Support and Family Peer Support Specialists often work in conjunction with a clinical team or mental health provider to help engage individuals with treatment and provide the additional support that individuals and their families need while trying to navigate the behavioral health system and other systems they may be involved with. Peer Support is an evidence-based practice shown to extend clinical impacts and increase engagement with those who would otherwise decline help and treatment.

I became a Certified Peer Support Specialist several years after my attempt. This has given me opportunities to assist others who struggle with similar challenges. This has had a very empowering and healing effect on me. If you are interested in becoming a peer support and/or family peer support, please check with your State's Department of Health and Human Services and/or Division of Substance Abuse and Mental Health Services for information on training and certification.

RESOURCES

U.S. Department of Health and Human Services/Substance Abuse and Mental Health Services Administration
https://www.samhsa.gov/brss-tacs/recovery-support-tools/peers
National Association of Peer Supporters
https://www.peersupportworks.org/
Copeland Center for Wellness and Recovery
https://copelandcenter.com/our-services/certified-peer-specialist-training-cps

All the links found in this book will be posted on my website for easy access
www.thrivingaftersuicideattempt.com

PARTING WORDS

My hope is that you will find at least one resource here that will help you on your personal journey, whether you are someone struggling with a mental illness or you are trying to help someone who is struggling.

Recovery is not one and done. It is a lifelong journey that takes place one day, one step at a time. Each individual and family is different. What works for one person may not work for another. The mental health landscape is constantly changing. The help and support a person can access in one geographic area may not be available in another. That's why it is so important to learn all you can about your loved one's mental health condition and the resources available in your area.

For a long time I didn't know that I had a mental illness and then when I found out I did, I didn't want anyone else to know. I wished I didn't have it. I wanted it to go away. I didn't know that there were resources, treatments, and support that I could tap into that would not only help treat my mental illness, but would actually empower me to learn and grow stronger because of it.

My mental illness has profoundly impacted my life but it does not define who I am as a person. I am not mentally ill. I have a mental illness. There is a big difference in that. Once your mental illness is acknowledged, embraced and addressed through support and helpful resources, you too will understand that you have the power to rise above one of life's most challenging circumstances.

I invite you to visit my website, www.thrivingaftersuicide attempt.com, to learn more about the resources available to you and/or your loved one. On my website, I provide links to all the resources in this book and will add new ones as I learn about them. You can contact me through my website if you have additional questions or something specific you would like to discuss that hasn't been covered here. I am also available to speak to groups at either in person or virtual events.

NOTES

NOTES

NOTES

NOTES

NOTES

NOTES

NOTES

NOTES

Made in the USA
Columbia, SC
04 September 2022

6647008 7R00136